VISIONS OF THE RAPTURE AND UNSEEN REALM

While Experiencing a Life Similar
to Job's and Visions Beyond the Veil,
an Angel Showed Me the Rapture.

G L E N D A   D U M A S

BALBOA
PRESS

A DIVISION OF HAY HOUSE

All of the Bible references were taken from the following on Biblegateway. com (spellings and verses were not changed or modified).

Balboa Press books may be ordered through booksellers or by contacting:

Balboa Press
A Division of Hay House
1663 Liberty Drive
Bloomington, IN 47403
www.balboapress.com
1 (877) 407-4847

Print information available on the last page.

ISBN: 978-1-5043-6805-6 (sc)
ISBN: 978-1-5043-6807-0 (hc)
ISBN: 978-1-5043-6806-3 (e)

Library of Congress Control Number: 2016916856

Balboa Press rev. date: 11/29/2016

To Alex, Nicole, and Alex Jr. for your assistance,
encouragement, and patience during this journey…

CONTENTS

*"The law and the prophets were until
John: since that time the kingdom of God is
preached, and every man presseth into it"
(Luke 16:16).*

Acknowledgement

Prophecy in the News
Oklahoma City, OK 73151
A special thank you to Mrs. Linda Church

Editors:

Nicole Harrison Obie

Adam Shapiro
Adam Shapiro Public Relations

Karen Summers
Summers Editorial Services

Attorney James W. Swindell

Art:

Michael Daughtry

Alex Harrison, Sr.

Sign Mine
Sign Mine, Inc.
High Point, NC 27265

INTRODUCTION

As a Christian, I must inform you that I do not believe in spirituality. My belief, as a Christian, is to maintain a strong adherence to biblical principles and to live my life accordingly. Most Christians believe that the dead are in the grave and cannot hear, see, or speak until the day of resurrection. When one talks of communicating beyond the veil, some people assume that is a form of spirituality. The Bible does mention the story of the rich man and Lazarus who could see and hear each other after their deaths as one was in Abraham's Bosom and the other in Hell. Believe me when I state that I do not have all of the answers. I do, however, try to convey my dreams and visions to you as I heard and saw them. In all things, give glory to the God of Abraham, Isaac and Jacob and ask of Him in the name of our Lord and Savior Jesus Christ to give you understanding as you read. I believe that I was chosen to deliver these messages because of my naivety. I was without a mentor or someone to guide me or interject their opinions as the visions began to materialize. Therefore, I could only convey my messages as I experienced them. A few of these visions and dreams may have my interpretation, but I have tried to let you know that this is what "I" was feeling, and my explanations are written as truthfully as I can remember them. I pray that you may understand the sincerity of each vision as I was seeing them and the internal conflicts that were raging in me to understand.

The term Rapture is not in the Bible. It is defined as the Lord taking his saints out of the earth to be with him while judgements inundate people left here. The Lord God saved Noah and his family from a flood, and He will save his saints from the tribulation that is to soon come. The saints will be taken to live with God until our Lord and Savior, Jesus Christ, comes back to rule and reign with his saints. It is shocking to note the number of people who continue to jeopardize their lives to live with our Savior as they break down the doors to go to Hell. Make a decision today as to where you want to spend eternity. This book gives you an insight to both places.

Imagine looking down on a globe displaying land masses and bodies of water. The globe's land masses are then populated with people of different colors, religions, and cultures. The globe can be concealed by using a thin cloth that filters in the light and absorbs the darkness. The atmosphere and the people can be influenced by manipulating this cloth. The cloth can be lifted from either side to allow entities or objects that can bring change. The cloth can also be lifted to allow people from the outside to peep in and people on the inside to peep out. People on the outside may peep in at the people on the inside to manipulate their lives. People on the inside may peep out into space, Heaven, Hell, another world, galaxy or alternate earth. This cloth is my representation of the veil that is covering the earth to prevent people who live here from peeping out and viewing otherworldly details before it is time. The earth is a part of the universe. We are situated in the Milky Way Galaxy. However, there are many galaxies that make up the world around us. Maybe, just maybe, someone or something can slip in and out of these portals that connect our parallel worlds. When the worlds connected, the veil lifted and I was allowed to peep over on the other side. If I was privileged to peep over and observe the outside, one must know for a fact that someone or something can peep over from the outside to observe us. Please know that you are being watched.

For those of you who love horror, you will love reading this book. My life has been more of a horror story or movie. And, it is real. One must, also, note that there are only two places to go once you leave this earth. They are Heaven or Hell. I pray daily for those of you who have chosen the wrong path in life. It is not too late to make a change. Remember, God is a forgiving God who gives us many chances.

Everyone can feel a change in the air. People are vicious. Indiscriminate killings and terrorism are threatening. There are changes in the climate with natural disasters belting the earth with a ferociousness that most of us have not seen before and it is utterly frightening. People are flabbergasted and asking the questions such as, what's happening, what's wrong, when will it stop, how did we get here, and how do we get out? Some give up on life and look for death. Others look to the Lord, the Rapture, and the end of days as stated in the Bible. There are many books on the Rapture and the end of days, but I don't think anyone has seen "how" it will happen. I have.

WHY ME?

A veil or covering keeps the people on earth from looking into other dimensions. I don't know exactly what it is or what it is made of at this time. However, I do know that someone is watching us and taking notes on the things that we do and say. Our very thoughts are also recorded somewhere out there beyond the veil. Yet, at times the veil opens, and angels and demons may slip through. Angels may come with messages to help or warn us. Demons come to harass, intimidate, and harm us. They have a resolve to do everything in their power to deny our entry into heaven to be with our Lord and Savior Jesus Christ. Most of you should be mindful of what is waiting for us beyond the veil. We are to know right from wrong, but most of us don't show it. There is definitely someone watching us. However, we choose to believe and live as though we are the masters of our fate. Where are you going?

The last days of man's quest for peace on this earth are coming to an end. The stage has been set for Armageddon to take place. This is the war that the Bible states is the last and most horrific battle that will involve Israel, and end in the return of our Lord and Savior Jesus Christ to set up His kingdom on earth. The violence and horrors that take center stage each day here on earth have signaled that the time is near. The villain, the deceiver in the form of the Antichrist, is about to take a bow. The Antichrist is the world leader that will bring the world to this last battle as he lays out the plans for the tribulation of the time that is about to emerge from this increasingly violent world.

Many established prophecy teachers know the Bible and have an audience for their words of knowledge. Many books have been written about God, Jesus Christ, the end-times, angels, and demons. We also have the Bible, which has been the standard for Christian believers. The Bible gives a history from the beginning of life: the redemption of man by Jesus Christ, and the time of God's judgments that are to befall His rebellious children. For many years, I have relied on my Bible, pastor, and prophecy teachers on the television to help me understand the messages of Christ and the prophets. However, I never imagined that I would be favored to witness the awesome power of our Lord and Savior. Therefore, I must explain all of the negativism that I encountered before yielding to the Lord and completing this book.

I love the Lord, but I am not a preacher with a huge congregation. I don't hold an office in my small town, and some people have never heard of me. However, the Lord allowed me to observe the manner in which the Rapture will take place by being transported into the future. I actually saw three visions that I attribute to the Rapture; witnessed horrifying visions from beyond the veil; survived being transported into towns populated by demons, and so have a better understanding of Satan's world; and witnessed angelic and demonic activity. To my knowledge, I don't recall anyone, or any books or movies, having this type of understanding about the Rapture. I devote most of my writing to the Rapture because this event was life-changing for me and was actually my first life-changing vision. I must warn you that this book is not for the fainthearted. However, if you love horror stories, please read my true story. Lastly, if you love the Lord, I believe that you will understand and believe my message.

A lesson learned: we have control over demonic activity or influences in our lives because demons can't control us if we don't let them. I realized very quickly that they are afraid of people who are truly filled with the love of God. The main role of demons is to intimidate us and make us afraid. Satan and his demons will flee us if we don't give them an audience. Will you try it and give the Lord a chance? I did by filling my life with the Holy Spirit and allowing Him to control my daily activities.

In this book, I address the dreams and visions that the Lord has given to me. I use biblical verses to explain what the Lord has shown me because the Bible explains itself very well. There may be repetition of verses and statements because this book began as a narrative and was presented in the order in which I received these visions, and later I organized the material for a book. Please know that I am continuously adding information as I receive it until publication. I try to be very precise and descriptive in the documentation of these dreams and visions and offer some explanations as to their meaning as the Lord leads me. Also, I want to make it clear to my reader that I am not really differentiating between the terms dreams and visions, because I don't know the difference according to the Bible's usage.

"For God speaketh once, yea twice, yet man perceiveth it not.
"In a dream, in a vision of the night, when deep sleep falleth upon men, in slumberings upon the bed" (Job 33:14–15).

The book of Job above states how God speaks to man. There can be no doubt that God speaks to us through dreams and visions of the night when one is in deep sleep or slumbering (napping). I want to state that I view some dreams as random occurrences of things that happen to us. Some dreams can be a rambling collage of the day's or past days' memories. Conversely, a vision is an occurrence that has meaning and in which one is physically present. A person has a mental picture of everything that goes on, although there may not be a clear understanding at the time. One's cognitive skills or mental abilities to think, analyze, or process these visions are at their highest level, as though one is awake. I often experience pain, touch, and smell in visions. Also, time continuum is definite in a vision. Visions are of the moment, and one's body is physically present in a vision. Visions may also occur during the dream stage of sleep. I must admit that I just don't know the Bible's definition of dreams and visions but have tried to convey a meaning through my personal experiences because I was asked to give a definition by an acquaintance.

I use the terms interchangeably because the Bible states that messages come from the Lord through dreams and visions. I really don't have a definitive explanation for either term and will use them as stated. I do, however, know when I am having a regular dream during the night, and I can differentiate between visions that I receive from the Lord. I actually state in one of my visions, "I am in a vision." In my visions, I am aware of what is happening around me and to people who are asleep in the house. All of my visions have truly captured my mind and heart. I truly feel blessed.

I must admit I was hesitant and confused about these visions when they started coming to me. I prayed and cried for answers, and continue to ask the question, "Why me?" I am a Christian, and I love the Lord with all of my soul. I know for a fact that Jesus Christ is my Savior and my Redeemer for me to enter heaven. However, I remain in awe of searching for an answer as to why I was chosen to witness these visions: how the Rapture will take place; a waiting area outside of heaven for the dead; diversities in demons; and, a vision of my Lord and Savior, Jesus Christ. While being troubled for several years about the vision of the Rapture and more, my reluctance intensified when I received a day, not the date, but a day for the Rapture. Please understand that I am not setting a date. Do not let this message of a day encourage anyone to consider setting a date for the Rapture. This is not my purpose. Let me add here that Satan knows what is happening in his world (earth), and he tries to counterfeit God's actions by inserting his thoughts in our dreams. Again, I am not setting a date, and neither should you.

In any case, I decided to share my messages with family and friends. Some of my family was hesitant at first, but soon realized that something was going on that could not be explained through normal processes. My friends began to look at me differently and made no comment. I shared the fact with them that I was receiving some of the same messages as a couple of evangelists on television. One of my friends stated that she doesn't look at the evangelists on television. I don't know why, because I can truly state that for all of you who don't watch a couple of these shows that I would recommend, you are missing out on a tremendous amount of history and knowledge. Some of these people research ancient manuscripts and are very knowledgeable of the past as it relates to scripture. There are several shows that I never miss and totally enjoy watching for the news and history lesson. Also, a number of these evangelists are stating that this is the time for the Lord to reveal His mysteries to His church. And, the Lord is choosing the people He wants to deliver His message. Also, I must note, some of us are seeing the same visions. For me, that is confirmation that what I am witnessing is true.

Please understand that I am an educated person. My visions are very vivid and very real. One day, I thought it would be nice to have the entire family see the things that my children and I are seeing. I really wanted the rest of my family to be witnesses with us. Therefore, I prayed and asked the Lord to let some of my family members see some of these visions and dreams. First, I had them to fast, pray together, and take communion each day. As of September 13, 2010, some of my relatives are now witnesses to visions too. We are dreaming dreams, seeing visions, and hearing things that are miraculous. Some of us are witnessing odd occurrences during the day while we are awake. Therefore, we know that we are not delusional and suffering from some form of sleep deprivation. These visions are real, and one doesn't have to be asleep to see them. I am truthful when I state, "We would not make these stories up." These are dreams and visions that we are seeing, and now are warning you of the imminence of the Rapture. This has got to be one reason for the Lord to allow us to be witnesses to these visions because we have nothing to gain for ourselves by inventing stories about the Lord God and our Savior Jesus Christ. In fact, I think that anyone who is bold enough to invent lies about the Bible or Jesus Christ may be doomed with the rest of an unbelieving world. People, please believe me: I have nothing to gain but everything to lose by inventing lies. I could lose my soul, and I am not trying to do that. I am telling you a truth that the Lord has allowed me to see, and about which to testify. And I have written this material in this book and described it as accurately as I remember. I would imagine a person would be doomed to hell if he or she were to invent lies about dreams or visions similar to what I have seen.

Believe me, I am too afraid of the visions that I have seen to lie about them: the good and the bad. Also, I don't think anyone could invent stories that you are about to read. My daughter and I were shown godly miracles and satanic occurrences as they relate to the world. I will not try to discuss the visions that others have seen. However, we were allowed to observe both worlds in our dreams and visions.

I found that a number of people don't believe in the Rapture. People believe in the supernatural power of demons and paranormal activity. Why is it difficult to get people to believe in the powers of God? There are too many people who try to challenge the powers and wonders of God and correlate them with some natural occurrence to make the Bible's statements appear less significant. Believe me, the God of Abraham is in the miracle-working business, and we are about to witness all of His power.

This is my testament to the visions that I saw. My apprehension continues to grow as I write the visions down and actually see them on paper. I also contacted several television evangelists and asked them for help because of my lack of expertise. The response was as expected. One program tried to assist me in identifying one of their programs that featured a woman who saw the same thing that I saw in heaven. Another program, *Prophecy in the News,* with Dr. J. R. Church and Gary Stearman, gave me permission to use quotes from its monthly magazine. I want to personally thank Mrs. Linda Church at this time for being so helpful.

After years of being troubled in my mind, I finally submitted to the Lord and asked Him to be my guide after encountering doubt from people who know me, and people I thought may have been as overwhelmed with this information as I. It is very difficult to change people's attitudes about beliefs that are well established in their minds and hearts from years of being educated in their various faiths. I am sincere when I state, "I am not trying to change anyone's beliefs." I am, however, trying to share with you the visions that the Lord has shown me. I feel as though I am encountering brick walls as I try to get my message to people who can make a difference, but as the Bible says, "Christians are long-suffering." And believe me, I am suffering to get this message out. I don't know if the people who have seen this manuscript believe in the Rapture or disbelieve in me. This undertaking has truly been a challenge.

It took some time for me to realize that this book is something that I have got to take charge over and get it out to the world. The Lord, also, reminded me that Jesus spoke in parables because His message was not for everyone when He came to the earth. Similarly, my message may not be for everyone either. Therefore, before you condemn me, please know who you are with the Lord.

As I continue to write, I gain information that I don't remember writing. I also lose information when I try to put too much of me and my thoughts into this book. At one point, I lost sixty pages in one week. As this continues to occur, it is my belief that I have divine assistance in writing this book. Believe me when I state that one publisher looked at me and said, "No one is going to believe you when you make statements like that: God giving you something to write?" Anyway, this is my belief; it may not mean anything to you. Again, I am not a biblical scholar, but

I read my Bible daily and pray that I am worthy. People, I am not under any influence other than the Lord. I want to be His messenger. I am filled with the fire of the Lord, and I want to share a message with you.

With many prayers and family supporters, I have grown stronger, and feel that I am now ready to reveal the visions that the Lord has given to me. I think this is my assignment, to let the world know what to expect. I can truly say that I have submitted to the Lord, and I am prepared to take on any critics. I consider myself a warrior for the Lord because many of the things that I saw in visions are happening now, and only the Lord could have shown me these visions before they happened.

> *"At that time Jesus answered and said, I thank thee, O Father, Lord of heaven and earth, because thou hast hid these things from the wise and prudent, and hast revealed them unto babes" (Matthew 11:25).*

Some prophets, preachers, and teachers profess to know all there is to know about our Lord and Savior. However, many things that are hidden from the wise and prudent are being revealed unto babes. I don't consider myself to be a babe in the natural sense, but I do consider myself to be a neophyte or novice as I try to relate my knowledge about the visions and dreams that I am experiencing. Moreover, I continue to ask, "Why me?"

Several friends read my manuscript and stated that I would have trouble convincing others of my visions because they felt that everything God wanted us to know was already written and was in the Bible. They stated, "The Bible is it. There is nothing new to write about! God is not raising up any new prophets." I agree that I am quite baffled by these revelations that I have been privileged to see. However, I do know that I purposely sought the Lord by fasting and praying, and I think He answered me with these dreams and visions. One may also have a problem with me stating that I saw these visions because I am not a preacher or prophet. With that said, let me remind you that Jesus did not choose a rabbi or a religious man to follow Him while He walked on earth. In addition, I draw a comparison for the reader by using Bible verses as the Lord leads me (a noted Christian author told me that I would have trouble convincing people of my visions by using this kind of language). I don't know any other language to use, other than to tell you the truth as I saw it and not by my interpretation. Additionally, we are to know when the Rapture and tribulation are near, according to the Bible. If we are to know this, I do believe that the Lord will let some of us see, hear, and identify the time, which I believe is now. Lastly, if my friends' statements are true, then Acts 2:17 would not be true for the last days.

> *"And it shall come to pass in the last days, saith God, I will pour out of my Spirit upon all flesh: and your sons and your daughters shall prophesy, and your young men shall see visions, and your old men shall dream dreams" (Acts 2:17).*

> *"Behold, I shew you a mystery; We shall not all sleep, but we shall all be changed" (1 Corinthians 15:51).*

I really don't know where to begin this book. Therefore, I will start with the most exciting and life-changing vision that I saw: the Rapture and some background information. The word *rapture* is not in the Bible. Paul describes it as a mystery above in 1 Corinthians 51. Our bodies will be changed, in a moment, in the twinkling of an eye, and at the last trump. In other words, those of us who will be taken in the Rapture will not die. We will be given new bodies and will be taken to heaven. Brothers and Sisters in Christ, this is exactly what I saw. It is an event that will happen to believing Christians who will be taken out of this world miraculously by the Lord before the tribulation described in the book of Revelation takes place. This is my definition of the Rapture, or the mystery that Paul reveals to Christians. Again, let me emphasize that I am not a prophecy teacher. I am conveying a message to you and describing it as best I can.

I have heard it stated that no man will know the day or the hour of the Rapture. So, I keep asking myself, "Why?" I pondered all of these feelings of inadequacies for years trying to justify why I was chosen as a messenger for the Lord. As I consider my life and all of my many trials, I keep coming back to the question, "Am I worthy of this task?" I did not get an answer, but the visions continue to come. Again I ask, "Is this woman from North Carolina qualified to be a messenger for the Lord?" As I contemplated this question and posed it to one of my brothers, he reminded me this: "Why not you? Remember the Azusa Street Revival was started in Los Angeles on the West Coast. Why shouldn't you be given the vision of the Rapture here on the East Coast? You are an avid reader of the Bible, and you study it as much as preachers and other scholars. Yet, these same preachers assume to know everything about the history of the church and do not. You pray and take communion every day. Do you not believe that God hears you? And, if He hears you, He may have found favor in you."

For anyone who is not familiar with the Azusa Street Revival, let me note that it was a driving force for the Pentecostal movement in the early 1900s. I look at it as an effort to draw people's attention to the day of Pentecost as it occurred when the Holy Spirit came upon the followers of Jesus Christ. It was one of the vehicles for the movement to be revived in the United States. I don't believe most preachers have heard of the Azusa Street Revival, because I have never heard a sermon about it. You may want to read information about this revival at some later time.

I notice most preachers that I know don't talk about visions or the Rapture, preach on the book of Revelation, or discuss demons in detail. My question to them is this, "How can you believe and preach on certain sections of the Bible and not all of it?" It is surprising for me to learn that most preachers don't believe in visions or the Rapture; thus, one reason for not preaching about it. It is most disturbing to learn that most preachers do not teach from the book of Revelation, which is the Revelation of Jesus Christ. Are you, preachers, feeding your flocks with the entire word of the Bible? If you are not, you may want to reconsider.

PREPARE FOR VISIONS

Please note how Daniel prepared himself to see visions from the Lord:

"In those days I Daniel was mourning three full weeks.
"I ate no pleasant bread, neither came flesh nor wine in
my mouth, neither did I anoint myself at all, till three whole
weeks were fulfilled" (Daniel 10:2–3).

I believe that through my prayers and fasting, the Lord heard me and showed me these wonderful and mighty visions. I must note that I don't believe everyone has to fast in the same manner. It took a number of years to get me to this point of spirituality, but, at least, I have finally conformed to His will, and my habits are more attuned to His ways. All one has to do is to be diligent with honesty and love abiding in one's heart while seeking Him, and He will answer. In addition, I fasted for many days while I was seeking the Lord's guidance while working on this book. And the visions continue to this day. I think it also matters what type of fasting one does to really see and hear great things from the Lord. I did what I have heard some preachers call a Daniel fast. Daniel fasted for twenty-one days, not eating or drinking anything with sugar (my interpretation), nor did he drink any wine or strong drink (my interpretation), nor did he eat any meat (my interpretation). The Lord communicates with us through visions, dreams, and angelic messages. How many of us take the time to hear from the Lord or put forth an honest effort to do so?

"Can a maid forget her ornaments, or a bride her attire?
yet my people have forgotten me days without number."
(Jeremiah 2:32).

Christians are the first people at church on Sunday to pray, sing, and worship the Lord. Let me tell you a secret: the Muslims pray each and every day to their God and several times throughout the day. The God of Abraham, Isaac, and Jacob states it very clearly in Jeremiah 2:32 that His people have forgotten Him days without number. The Lord is worthy of our prayers and seeks to give us His blessings. It is sad that our Lord is forgotten day after day, without His people giving Him prayers and praises.

The Lord is asking us to remember Him. One way to remember Him is by fasting and prayer. How many of us get up and thank the Lord for letting us see a new day? How many of us pray in the morning and at night for our families and friends? The Lord wants us to pray to Him; this is our way to talk to Him, and He answers.

My First Vision of the Rapture

It was Saturday, March 26, 2005, that I saw my first vision of the Rapture. This date is very significant for me and my family because my mother died on March 27, 2004. The date of the vision was almost a year from the day that my mother died; my daughter brought this fact to my attention. The Lord operates in dates and times. I still get chills as I repeat what I saw. My head was motionless on my pillow. The vision began with me, my daughter, and my two sisters standing outside of my mother's house. One of my sisters and my daughter left us to go inside of a neighbor's home. Everything around us was calm, and there was no warning of harm or any type of calamity befalling the earth. It was a normal day, and all of us were at peace and had no worry. We appeared to be going out into the neighborhood to talk to our neighbors or just stand around outside and talk as we normally do. For some reason, the sister with me and I looked to the sky. We did not hear or see anything unusual, but we looked to the sky. It was a deep blue, crisp sky with two small snowy white clouds scattered about. It was a deep dark blue that was not obscured by any smog. It was a dark blue sky that one sees sometimes in the fall as the heat of the summer is fading, or perhaps the vibrant, brilliant, deep blue sky of spring that is getting ready for the heat of the summer. Even now, I tend to shudder and await a presence in the sky when I see this color of blue as I look to the sky each day. Suddenly, the blueness of the sky started to swirl as though something was making ripples or swirling motions in the air. A translucent planet similar to the earth appeared: it was the outline of another world skillfully placed against the deep blue sky. It was translucent in the sense that there appeared an outline of a planetlike object in the sky. It did not have the land mass and topography that the earth has; but it was another world nonetheless and was very similar to earth as seen from space, but without visible outlines of islands showing. The planet appeared to have pear-shaped north and south land outlines that were connected by a small strip of outline that may have been a landmass. It also had well-defined continuous borders on either side of these presumed landmasses that ran from north to south. We stood there hypnotized at the sight of this earthlike sphere, trying to figure out what it was. Our minds and every thought transfixed in our heads as to what this could possibly be that suddenly appeared out of seemingly nothing but the deep space.

Before I could speak a word, my sister said, "Look, there's a hand!" The hand was very real and as translucent as the planet that we were seeing. It appeared as an outline of a hand just sitting in space to the left and just below the translucent planet. In the next second, the hand was completed with the solid features of an enormous man, which I identified as an angel of the Lord clothed in a robe down to his feet, which was girded about the waist with a thin rope-like item. He literally filled the sky and was taller than any building or mountain that I have seen on the earth. There was the angel of the Lord with a light-colored ram's horn or shofar, immediately putting it to his mouth to summon the saints to heaven for the Rapture. Yes, I said the shofar, the Jewish religious horn that is blown to bring the Jews to services. Yes, I said the Jews because the Jews are God's chosen people, and Jesus was a Jew.

The angel or person that I saw was dressed in a long light-colored robe. I can't remember at this time whether it was bound with a tie at the waist, but since I wrote this down some time ago, as stated above, I will not make any changes to the first statement. See the importance of writing down the vision and making it plain as the Lord demands. He had a small band around his forehead and hair. I did not see any wings, and I did not hear the sound that the shofar made. I turned to see where my sister and daughter were at this time. My sister and the people who were standing with her shrank in a second, the twinkling of an eye, and were no more. That is how it happened. First they shrank, clothes and all that they had on them, and, suddenly, they were gone! Let me note here: Jesus was resurrected and left behind his burial clothes, according to the Bible. He had to ascend to God before He could be touched. The raptured saints will have glorified bodies immediately because Jesus has paid the price, and they will be taken directly up, clothes and all. Remember—Paul said we will be changed. I will talk about this later.

This all happened suddenly. Yes, in the twinkling of an eye. My daughter and the sister who was with me did not go up either. There was an instant message placed on my heart and mind that "I could have gone if I had forgiveness and love in my heart." Evidently, most people on earth are also as unforgiving as I was because I did not see many people going up. Please understand. I did not see many people going up in the Rapture! It is frightening to know that many of us will be left here after the Rapture. Church membership cannot prepare you to go up. Only a Christlike love and forgiveness will allow you to be Raptured.

The angel spoke to me through telepathy. His words were just there in my head, and my words were transmitted back to him in the same manner. Please note, I just heard a preacher on television saying that he communicated in the same manner with Jesus and angels. At any rate, the angel looked at me with very sad eyes. I call him an angel or messenger; I don't know which he is at this time and will pose a question to you later in this book, because he did not identify himself. I pray that God will let me know who he is because he did not have wings like those of an angel that I could see. I answer this later in the book because I, now, know who he was.

Suddenly, my body seemed to have been transported to his line of sight, and our eyes were staring at each other. He had eyes that had seen pain and suffering firsthand. Eyes that stared at me, that looked through me, down to my very soul. They were eyes that showed a hurt that the sands of time could not contain. They were eyes that were sad for me and all of the people who did not hear the sound of the shofar: my sister and daughter are included. They were scolding eyes; eyes that one often sees when parents are disgusted with you. Eyes that tell you without speaking that you have done wrong and sinned against the Most High God. Eyes that say, "You should have been listening; you should have studied; and, you should have known that this day was coming." Eyes that say, "Why weren't you prepared?" Eyes that say, "It is too late." Eyes that say, "What have you done with your time?" And eyes that state that you were not about your Father's work. Eyes that appeared grieved for all of the lost souls that were left here; eyes that did all the talking without mouth or lips moving;

eyes that remind me of my mother when she would look at us, her children, when we had done something wrong when we were little and say, "Didn't I tell you better?" They were eyes that spoke words even though no sound could be heard; eyes that spoke to my soul while telling me that it was too late for me to go up; eyes that cried out in pain, asking, "Why didn't you practice what you preached?"

The angel (yes, he was an angel) stated this simple message that I have for all of you who read this book: "You must forgive, and love everyone." It doesn't matter who you know and meet. All people are to be loved by you: your family, friends, enemies, and people who misuse you and abuse you. This means everyone. Let me state this again. I saw the swirling air in the sky, the planet, the hand, and then the angel of the Lord blowing the shofar. His message was to forgive and to love. I already know that I am a child of God, but it is so easy to slip into unforgivingness. That simple little slip may cost you your soul. I could love, but I could not forgive. Isn't that a simple message for Christians? We already know the Lord God and His Son Jesus Christ, but we have forgotten His message to forgive and to love. I was grieving the Holy Spirit by keeping unforgiveness in my heart. Remember—Christian brothers and sisters, that our bodies are the temples of the Holy Spirit. If you are harboring unforgivingness in your hearts, you can't love your brothers. Please stop it now! The message was for me to go to the people that I was not forgiving, and I knew exactly who they were. I truly believed that I had not done anything wrong, and it was these people that I thought owed me an apology, or that needed to reach out to me and ask for my forgiveness. Nevertheless, I realized that it was me who was letting this unforgivingness rule my days and my nights. I was hurt by them and their actions, and I wanted them to know it. Let me state for the record that I went to all of their houses (three different houses) that day to tell them that I love them and that I forgive them. I was that frightened, and I was moved by the message to do so that day. I pray that you are moved in the same manner.

Forgive and *love*, these are two powerful words. They are simple words that have powerful meanings. When I was left here, I told the angel, "That's easy. I can forgive and love now." He told me that it was too late. This terrified me. Unforgivingness was making me think about what these people had done to me, and I couldn't forget it. Anyway, these are two very simple words that demand a simple act on our behalf. This is not hard to do when you think about the consequences. Do it now because it will be too late when the shofar blows.

> *"For the Lord himself shall descend from heaven with a shout, with the voice of the archangel, and with the trump of God: and the dead in Christ shall rise first"* (1 Thessalonians 4:16).

Notice the above verse that states that the Lord will descend with the voice of the archangel and the trump of God. The archangels mentioned in the King James Bible are Michael and Gabriel. I believe Satan was an archangel at one time, but he lost his position when he rebelled against God. Although, there are seven archangels mentioned in the book of Enoch that most people identify with the angels in the Bible. Could this angel be one of them? Just a thought because I don't know.

The next thing that I remember seeing after the angel had blown the shofar and the Rapture had taken place was a murder. Thievery was the second thing that I saw. A murder occurred, and the person's weapon that she had for protection was stolen. The book of Revelation explains all of the events that will happen after the Rapture. It is interesting to note Revelation 9:21.

> *"Neither repented they of their murders, nor of their sorceries, nor of their fornication, nor of their thefts"* (Revelation 9:21).

Lord God, help us! Only through the Lord Jesus Christ can we be saved and not be here to witness and become a victim of an increasingly mad world. Revelation 9:21 happens sometime after the Rapture of God's saints. I believe the only saints left after the Rapture are 144,000 Jews who have the seal of God in their foreheads. They will be supernaturally protected here on the earth. After the Rapture, the first thing that I saw happen was a murder, just as verse 21 states above. The second thing that I saw was a theft. I am using these verses to explain what I saw. People are going to be in such absolute horror and confusion because some will be aware that the Rapture has taken place, and they will be upset and angry that they did not go. Still others will be ignorant of the fact of the Rapture and will look to cause harm or danger to anyone who gets in their way. Whatever you have, they will want. Whatever is yours will become theirs. Mayhem and bleak futures loom for those who are left.

I remember looking at the person who was murdered. I felt helpless. Then it dawned on me that I needed to get to the rest of my family and find safety. I needed to know who was left. My family and I found it difficult to travel and communicate with family members after the Rapture. I don't know why, but I could sense that there was some type of disruption in the lines of communication: satellite systems, telephones, and cell phones. Also, for some reason, we were walking and not driving to check on our families. Oil shortages may cause a problem with transportation. If the oil stops flowing, we will be walking. I did not see any planes falling from the sky, or train or car wrecks, because I was basically in my neighborhood and did not venture far. And, let me add, I don't know if these things will happen. I only know that it was as the Lord said that it would be in the end-times. As in the days of Noah, so are the days in which we live. Please note Genesis 6:11.

"The earth also was corrupt before God, and the earth was filled with violence" (Genesis 6:11).

The days of Noah, according to Genesis, were corrupt and filled with violence. Today, the earth is corrupt and filled with violence, and it is going to get worse. Isn't it amazing? The people of the world have not learned a lesson from the days of Noah to this day. It is time to repent, instead of being doomed to the same fate of the people in Noah's day. What kind of rescue do you want? After the Rapture happens, men will become exceedingly corrupt and filled with evil and thoughts of violence at every turn. Although the world as we know it is a very violent place today, imagine, if you will, it becoming hundreds of times worse in the aftermath of the Rapture.

Daniel's Interpretation of a Vision

L et's take a step back in time to note the vision of a prophet. This following vision in the book of Daniel happened while he was held captive in Babylon, which is in Iraq. Isn't it strange that we Americans are fighting a war there now? Daniel was a Jew and was most loved by God, as we can see in the scripture. I feel a strong connection between Daniel's vision and mine for some reason. My vision of the Rapture reminds me of Daniel 5:5, where King Belshazzar saw the writing on the wall. I now have a vivid image of what he saw, since my vision began with the air being troubled, the translucent earthlike planet, and then the translucent hand placed upon the background of a rich blue sky with two small snowy white clouds placing themselves to the left of the planet. I have often wondered whose fingers Belshazzar saw. For the Bible says: fingers of a man's hand wrote upon the plaster, and the king saw only the part of the hand that wrote. I won't go into any details about the writing on the wall, but you may read it for yourself.

King Belshazzar was having a feast. He and his guest were using the sacred vessels that were looted from the temple in Jerusalem to drink their wine. Note Daniel:

> "In the same hour came forth fingers of a man's hand,
> and wrote over against the candlestick upon the plaister of
> the wall of the king's palace: and the king saw the part of the
> hand that wrote" (Daniel 5:5).

This is really fascinating to me. Please bear with me for a moment. I don't know that it matters one way or the other. However, the Bible states emphatically that Belshazzar saw the fingers of a man's hand. This comes to mind again as I reminisce back to the outlines that I saw. The planet appears as a translucent sphere and then the translucent hand appears with no connecting body. They both were translucent with the planet showing outlines that may have been landmasses similar to the landmass of earth, while looking at North and South America as they are seen from space. Now, I must make a note here. I only saw an outline. The area that appeared to be similar to North and South America could have been landmasses or water. Also, the north and south areas had well-defined borders that were similar to inverted pear shapes (very similar to South America). Remember—everything was translucent. However, it did appear to be earthlike from the outline with northern and southern connecting masses. Also, there were no outlines protruding out like Florida or any of the islands and other landmasses like earth.

As I try to be clear about the vision, I am trying to explain as much to you as possible for my readers to have a vivid picture of what I saw. According to John 5:2–4, an angel would trouble the water in a pool by the sheep market in Jerusalem. It is described as a pool having five porches. A number of people who were blind or withered would lie in these porches in order to be healed. It is stated that an angel would go down and trouble the water, and the first person stepping into the water would be made whole of whatsoever disease he had.

Now, I can sit back and think. Did the fingers make the swirling motion in the sky before anything appeared? The fingers must have troubled the air before the planet could appear in the heavens. The fingers also must have made some path in the atmosphere for the angel. Could the hand that I saw be the same hand that Belshazzar saw thousands of years ago? Was the air troubled by the hand and made to look as though someone was stirring it? Was this similar to the way that the water in the pool in Jerusalem was troubled years ago as noted in John 5:2–4? It certainly looked as water that is stirred. Additionally, did the hand belong to the same man that I saw in the vision? I don't know, but I continue to pray and ask for understanding.

Let us examine the writing (not to interpret) on the wall in the book of Daniel. Daniel is one of many great prophets in the Bible that had wisdom of the end-time and could interpret dreams of someone else's after praying and believing in his God, the God of Abraham, Isaac, and Jacob. Note that the God of Daniel is the one who sets up rulers in the kingdom of men and appoints whomever He will to rule over it. Just a note: Isn't it a sad thought that politicians may have been set up by God, and they refuse to work with each other in a decent, godly manner? He set up Belshazzar also to use him to show His glory.

Again, Belshazzar, the king of Babylon, was having what we would call a party. He had a great feast prepared and much wine. At some point in this story, Belshazzar commands his servants to get the golden and silver cups that his grandfather had taken from the most Holy Temple of the Lord in Jerusalem. Just imagine that this man wanted to drink wine from the holy vessels that had been in the temple of God. This man had the nerve to think that his sins would not find him on that night. However, someone was watching him. I think that people who live here on earth are being watched, have been watched, and will continue to be watched and judged until the Rapture takes place. And, everyone will be judged just as Belshazzar was judged. Therefore, watch what you are doing. The Bible states very clearly that there are watchers, holy ones, and angels. Sometimes people tend to behave more appropriately when they know that someone is watching. Saints, Christians, and brethren, behave like you know that you are being watched by someone on high. Someone is looking beyond the veil at all times. Where are you going?

"Then was the part of the hand sent from him; and this writing was written" (Daniel 5:24).

Isn't this exciting? A hand appeared out of the air and wrote against a wall. The hand was sent from Him. I shiver when I think that the hand that I saw could have been that of the Most High God. Again, the heavenly messenger did not identify himself, but I do believe he was an angel. The importance of the hand writing on the wall was to show the power of the Lord and reveal His power through the interpretations that Daniel delivered.

Before Belshazzar had his vision, his grandfather, Nebuchadnezzar, had a dream, and the Lord gave Daniel the interpretation of that vision too. Please read the book of Daniel. He was a man who was very much loved by God. These dreams and visions can be baffling, for I suffered many nights before I decided, or the Lord put it on my heart, to write this book. I am probably writing this backward because Nebuchadnezzar came first and was Belshazzar's grandfather. Please note Nebuchadnezzar's dream by reading the book of Daniel.

Nebuchadnezzar's dream was troubling to him. Yet, he states that he forgot the dream by saying, "The thing is gone from me." I forgot some things too. However, Habakkuk 2:2 states to write the vision. We are to write down all visions that we receive from the Lord. This is for the purpose of others to read and for it to be a permanent document to last throughout time. Also, the vision can be forgotten and not brought back to memory if it is not recorded. However, I believe that it was God's will that the king forgot the dream so that Daniel could show the glory of God.

Daniel receives his message from the Lord God in night visions. You, too, can receive visions in the same manner if you ask and are a Christian and believe in your heart that you will receive an answer. People seek power, but I believe this is more powerful than anything on earth: to have a conversation with our Father God. The Lord God wants to talk to us. If He loved us enough to send His Son to die for us, please believe that He wants a relationship with His children.

Daniel and his friends became leaders over the affairs of the men in Babylon because Daniel was found worthy to interpret a dream for the king. I must also state that Daniel was given a vision of end-time prophecy: one reason for me including information about him. Just as there was a message for Belshazzar and his grandfather, Nebuchadnezzar, my vision has a message too. The message was for me to look at myself first and to find out what was wrong in the way that I was feeling. The heart can carry a heavy burden without us realizing that these burdens here on earth can't compare to the happiness that we will receive in heaven, if we can endure to the end. The end as I see it is the Rapture of the saints that will come when we are taken away from this mean and cruel world. To be raptured, all of us have to look first at ourselves and our hearts. We need to make a simple change just as I did. I did it that day. Sure, you will be tempted by people to change your heart and mind-set. However, stay the course and stay away from temptation. Some people are meant to be loved from a distance. You don't have to associate with them at all. Love them and keep your hearts and minds clean.

Again, the angel that I saw demonstrated that Christians who do not forgive and love will not go up in the Rapture of the church. Isn't that a simple request of us? Also, I could not hear the shofar as the angel blew it. I have no idea of the sound that it emitted. I could not hear it for I could not go up. I had to be a witness to inform the people that for all of you who are left, you will not hear a sound. And, I would imagine, too, that non-Christians who are left will not know where the people have gone that were taken up. I don't know if everyone will see the planet or the angel if they are not to go up. This is not clear at this time, and, as before, I don't want to assume. Although I can say this, my sister also saw the planet, the hand, and the angel. She did not go up either. It seems that both of us may have been dealing with forgiveness issues. My sister is a very loving and giving person and never speaks harshly to anyone, will not respond to hateful words, and is a loving Christian. I can understand me and my unforgivingness because it was true. Everything that the angel revealed was true. I don't remember my daughter stating that she saw the angel. Since she did not go up either, I imagine all of us had unforgivingness in our hearts. Therefore, this thought would lead one to believe that the people who are left may see the angel and not hear the shofar.

The people that we live with and share our lives with are some of the people who distract us the most. Family members tend to offend and cause us the most pain. You must forgive these people (all people) even though it may be difficult, especially since you are around family more than others. If it is possible, forgive them and love them from a distance. Do whatever is necessary to stay away from offenses.

On another note, I would like to address the planet again that I saw in the sky. I thought for a long time about this planet. I just could not understand why it appeared too. I imagined, and I really hate to assume something that is Bible related. I assume that this planet is the place that the people went to as they were called up. There is no other reason for the planet to appear at this particular time. Another thought is that the planet may be the visible sign that the Lord God Almighty has prepared a new heaven and earth, and this planet is the visible sign that the new earth is completed. Could this planet be a picture of heaven as it looks from space? At one time, I was telling my family and friends that this was the case. I was saying that I saw heaven, but that is not true. I think I wanted to see heaven and stated this. I may be assuming too much because I really don't know yet.

The book of Revelation mentions a new heaven and earth coming down from God in the last days. This body (bodies) has no seas. Now I am still left with a dilemma because the planet that I saw had what I thought to be a landmass and what appeared to be water or oceans (by comparing it to earth). Therefore, if there are no more seas in the new heaven and new earth, this planet that I saw could not possibly be the new heaven and the new earth. On the other hand, the area that I assumed to be the landmass may truly have been just that. And, the strong lines that I saw may have been divisions within the land itself instead of oceans. I don't really need to try to assume what it is, nor do I need to know exactly what it is. I think the angel would have told me of its importance if I really needed to know at that particular time, but he did not. Therefore, I really don't know what the earthlike planet was. Lastly, the people who are raptured have to go somewhere. Where do they go? Do they go to this planet? Is this the reason that I saw it?

My Second Vision of the Rapture

I continue to fast and pray, and I continue to have dreams and visions. During the last week of July 2007, I had another vision that I attributed to the end of days. I was in a hospital or some type of building that reminded me of a hospital. There were a number of windows and glass in the building including the ceiling and along the sides of the building's walls. As I and many others looked up through the glass in the ceiling, we saw hundreds of unidentified flying objects (UFOs) with bottle-neck tops and larger oval bottoms. They were golden metal UFOs hovering in formation one behind the other and side by side in the sky. There appeared to be white spikes (maybe landing gear) protruding out of the tops and bottoms. These ships appeared to be ready for combat, but I don't know if that was their purpose. I stated this because of the formation of the UFOs. For some reason, it reminded me of a military formation (my belief).

I have a question to pose to you. Do you believe that UFOs will appear and be associated with the Rapture? Is this a way that Satan and his agent, the Antichrist, will enter in on the scene? Here are my thoughts on this subject. I believe that UFOs will appear and give nonbelievers, who are left here on earth, a means to explain the missing people who are taken during the Rapture. This makes perfect sense to me that the UFO phenomenon may be exposed and received as a truth to explain the Rapture. After all of the years that people have experienced these flying marvels, they will be explained away as the mystery ships that took people during the Rapture. The Antichrist will be given a perfect alibi to explain away the Rapture and to make his case for world dominance. For he (the Antichrist) will not be revealed to the world until after the Rapture takes place, according to

Paul in 2 Thessalonians 2:2. That man of sin will not be revealed without the falling away, or the Rapture, happening first. This is my thought, only. Some prophets have different views of this "falling away" phenomenon. The Antichrist will be accepted as some sort of savior for mankind. This is the person who will control people, world governments, and most of the world leaders. He gains his power through Satan but calls himself God and will sit in God's temple. Be not deceived, brothers and sisters, for that day will come when the righteous are taken out of the way, and then the Antichrist will be revealed.

> *"For the mystery of iniquity doth already work: only he who now letteth will let, until he be taken out of the way.*
> *"And then shall that Wicked be revealed, whom the Lord shall consume with the spirit of his mouth, and shall destroy with the brightness of his coming" (2 Thessalonians 2:7–8).*

Christians who are filled with the Holy Spirit or the Church of Jesus Christ are the ones who will be taken during the Rapture. They are also the Christians who have love and forgiveness in their hearts. The Holy Spirit is the barrier that the Antichrist can't break (my thought). I believe that the Holy Spirit, which is the power that we received from God, is keeping the Antichrist in check for now until after the Rapture. He, the Holy Spirit, that is now "letteth" [sic] will let until he be taken out of the way according to 2 Thessalonians 2:7. I believe the Holy Spirit is the power that helped me to deal with my visions. The Holy Spirit will be taken away with the church during the Rapture. Again, these are my thoughts and interpretations about a statement that I've heard for years. A number of biblical scholars have noted the above in their interpretation of this passage too. However, in the past month, I've noticed that a couple of scholars are stating the "He" who letteth is Michael, the archangel. This may be true also because I think I saw an archangel, and it could have been Michael who blew the shofar. At any rate, for now, I will refer to the "he who now letteth" as the Holy Spirit because I just don't know at this point. Many interpretations of the Bible are on the market. This is the reason for every one of you who read this book to do your own research. As for me, when I don't know a statement is factual, I will let you know. I can only describe what I have seen, heard, and felt. Sometimes, feelings can get in the way and cause problems. However, I try to be as honest as possible.

Second Thessalonians 2:7 states that something or someone is keeping the Antichrist from being revealed until his time. The Disciples, who were filled with the Holy Spirit on the day of Pentecost, operated with an amazing power. I believe that the Holy Spirit has got to be the power that makes born again Christians know who they are in Christ. The Holy Spirit is the power (my thoughts). The Holy Spirit lives in all Christians who are living like Jesus Christ. For me, if the body of a believer goes, so does the Holy Spirit. After the Rapture, that Wicked will be revealed because the Holy Spirit or power is gone. Please note in 2 Thessalonians 2:8 that the Lord will consume the Wicked or Antichrist with the spirit of his mouth. Therefore, I feel that I am correct in stating the Holy Spirit abiding in believers is the power that is keeping the Antichrist from being revealed at this time. Again, these are my thoughts. I will expand on the Holy Spirit as the power later in this book. This may help one to understand why I strongly believe this statement.

Keep in mind the fact that scholars have strong opinions on this subject of "who is the person who "letteth," until he be taken out of the way. They believe that it is Michael the archangel instead of the Holy Spirit. Please note that I also believe I saw an archangel who blew the shofar before the Rapture. Therefore, their statement may be true too. We know that something is keeping the Antichrist at bay for the moment.

"And for this cause God shall send them strong delusion,
that they should believe a lie" (2 Thessalonians 2:11).

One wonders why some people will believe in this man and his lying wonders. Here is your answer. God shall send a strong delusion, that they should believe a lie, according to 2 Thessalonians 2:11. Do you understand? God will send a "strong" delusion to some of the people who are left to believe the lies of the Antichrist. The people who are left here are the ones who did not receive the love of truth. If these people had received the truth and lived Christlike, they would have been raptured. However, they preferred to be deceived and live unrighteous lives, according to 2

Thessalonians 2:10. For this reason, they will perish. One is playing with fire and might perish if he or she does not believe in the truth. Why not believe God before you are forced to believe a lie? Where are you going?

Brothers and sisters in Christ, we allowed God to be taken out of our schools. The Ten Commandments can't be displayed on government property. How did this happen to a country that was built on Christian values? On the other hand, was this a guise? Can you not believe that God will judge you for turning your back on Him? Be wary of people who call right wrong; and wrong right; or good evil; and evil good. If someone's talk and actions do not align with the commandments of God, then you should stay away from him or her. People are asking that laws be passed within states to change the beliefs that Christians have lived by for years eternal. I wonder if these people have been sent a strong delusion, that they should believe a lie! If something was wrong in the past, don't look to man and his laws to make it right for now. It was a lie then, and it is a lie now! If something was hidden in the past because it was considered wrong, people, think for yourselves. Who can make it right? Who can make it right if it is biblically wrong?

Hold fast to your biblical beliefs. Hold fast to the traditions of the Bible. Do not be misled by a lie. Man's laws can't replace God's laws. Judges can't replace biblical laws with a lie. Where are you going?

> *"For we wrestle not against flesh and blood, but against principalities, against powers, against the rulers of the darkness of this world, against spiritual wickedness in high places" (Ephesians 6:12).*

According to Ephesians 6:12, we wrestle with principalities, against powers, against the rulers of the darkness of this world, and against spiritual wickedness in high places. This verse clearly states that our battles are with the supernatural forces constantly at work. Our battles are with the supernatural forces on this earth. Most people do not accept the fact that this is Satan's world. Over the years, since I was a young girl, I have studied the pictures of the beings, aliens or extraterrestrials that supposedly came from UFOs. These beings are depicted on posters as short in height with big oval-shaped heads, large bulging eyes, and a slit for a mouth. I know that most of you have seen them. Does this description bring to mind anything in particular to you, my readers? How about reptiles or snakes or cobras?

I have a gnawing thought that has me wondering about the appearance of Satan. The Bible states that he is a serpent and a dragon. I want to note an article from *Prophecy in the News* magazine (Dr. J. R. Church, "The Ancient Book of Enoch," *Prophecy in the News*, March 2009, 38). According to an article that Dr. J. R. Church wrote on the ancient book of Enoch, he lists six watchers whom he calls "holy angels." They are listed as follows: "Uriel is in charge of earth's weather system; Raphael heads the department that records our thoughts and prayers. Raguel is in charge of our solar system; Sarqael maintains surveillance over the evil spirits who induce the 'children of men' to sin; Michael is in charge of defending the Chosen People (Israel); and Gabriel is in charge of the serpents, Paradise and the Cherubim who guard(ed) the Eastern Gate of Eden." Dr. Church goes on to state that Satan once held Gabriel's position as watcher over the serpents and that Satan is a serpent (the great red dragon, himself).

It is also interesting to note that Moses made a brass serpent for the Jews to look upon while in the wilderness to cure them from fatal serpent bites. Satan appeared to Adam and Eve, also, as a serpent. Therefore, I would say that it is not too hard on the imagination to assume that Satan and serpents may have some type of connection. Are Satan and the serpent the same in nature? Also, according to the Bible, some of the names of Satan are: devil, Lucifer, that old serpent, and dragon.

Another thought that puzzles me is the phenomenon of alien abduction. The *Prophecy in the News* magazine has an article of particular interest by Gary Stearman (Dr. J. R. Church and Gary Stearman, "Genetic Tampering, Ancient and Modern," *Prophecy in the News*, July 2010, 8). Please read it if you can get a copy. I often wonder why aliens would abduct humans. Who are these aliens? I believe they are the fallen angels who fell with Satan. There are many books on this subject, and I will not attempt to explain this any further. I have seen many movies and programs featuring people who claim to have been abducted by aliens. Sometimes they claim that the aliens performed experiments on their reproductive organs by implanting fetuses or taking fetuses out. I don't have any answers at this time.

Additionally, the phenomenon of UFOs makes sense, especially if it is true that these beings have been visiting people and subjecting them to all types of experiments as I and many of you have heard through the years. If Satan was in heaven and declared that he wanted to be God and led a full third of the angels with him to be spirits roaming the earth, then they are still here. He and his angels are here and have complete access to earth. Could these aliens be the fallen angels that were cast out of heaven, or some demon that they spawned? For the record, when people seek to conquer, just as Satan, they may attempt to have the human DNA to become more akin to their own or attempt to corrupt the human DNA. Isn't this what one of the most evil men in history tried to do too? I'm referring to Adolf Hitler. He wanted to make his super race of blonde blue-eyed people. Isn't this what some hate groups want? Some hate groups want a race of people that look like themselves, or a super race for themselves over which they can be sovereign. People, do you know what you are asking for? This is how Satan got started. Satan wanted to be in charge. Listen, please, all of the hate groups of the world, and reconsider your actions.

Please note, also, that scientists are manipulating DNA by cloning animals, people, and our food. Why? I have no idea. Satan was the master of cloning by allowing his angels to have relations with the women on earth, according to Genesis. Heaven only knows what they are up to now.

> *And it came to pass, when men began to multiply on the face of the earth, and daughters were born unto them,*
> *That the sons of God saw the daughters of men that they were fair; and they took them wives of all which they chose.*
> *And the LORD said, My spirit shall not always strive with man, for that he also is flesh: yet his days shall be an hundred and twenty years.*
> *There were giants in the earth in those days; and also after that, when the sons of God came in unto the daughters of men, and they bare children to them, the same became mighty men which were of old, men of renown.*
> *And God saw that the wickedness of man was great in the earth, and that every imagination of the thoughts of his heart was only evil continually (Genesis 6:1–5).*

Let me state that I am not an authority on any of these facts. Assume with me for a moment. We note in Genesis that the angels visited and mated with women on earth in the past and created great men or giant men. Taking note of these verses, it appears that these are the angels who followed and fell with Satan. Since Satan and these angels were in heaven with God, we can note that they had great knowledge about the world and the universe. They most likely shared this knowledge with the people on earth. With this knowledge, the people became very corrupt in the sight of the Lord, and He decided to destroy them through a flood. The race of beings that were created by them may have been partially destroyed. There existed giants in those days before and after the flood. The giants and the demons that they produced may be here to this day.

Again, isn't it interesting to note that people who say that they have been abducted by these extraterrestrial beings are saying that sexual experiments were conducted on them? Are Satan and his angels trying to create their race of giants again? I included the verses referring to this from the Bible. Sometimes facts from the Bible can appear too supernatural for some of us. However, it is there for you to see and believe. Note Genesis 6:1–5 again.

Now, please bear with my imagination for a moment. This is just me talking and wondering, "What if this is true?" Egypt was one of the first great kingdoms. Take a look at the gods of Egypt for a moment. I am only using Egypt as an example because most people are familiar with the country.

Egypt was one of the first and greatest empires, which lasted for many centuries. One of my brothers is a history enthusiast. He reminded me that, at some point in Egyptian history, the gods representing Upper and Lower Egypt were a vulture and a cobra. I just want to mention this here to make a point that most of us have seen the cobra on the top of King Tut's mask, and, through the years, many of the gods of Egypt were half human with animal features. I will not mention any of the gods by name here, but note that it may be of interest to you to research later. The Egyptian Empire was not that far removed from Noah and the flood. If evil angels were here on earth mating with women, one can believe that all kinds of offspring could have been produced. Let's lay some groundwork for the way that angels look.

"Also out of the midst thereof came the likeness of four living creatures. And this was their appearance; they had the likeness of a man.

"And every one had four faces, and every one had four wings" (Ezekiel 1:5–6).

"As for the likeness of their faces, they four had the face of a man, and the face of a lion, on the right side: and they four had the face of an ox on the left side; they four also had the face of an eagle.

"Thus were their faces: and their wings were stretched upward; two wings of every one were joined one to another, and two covered their bodies" (Ezekiel 1:10–11).

"And when they went, I heard the noise of their wings, like the noise of great waters, as the voice of the Almighty, the voice of speech, as the noise of an host: when they stood, they let down their wings" (Ezekiel 1:24).

As noted above, angels have many different appearances. They have the appearance of a man, lion, ox, and eagle. Their wings are described in great detail by Ezekiel. Their talk is like the noise of great waters, and they let down their wings when they stood. This is not what I saw. I saw a man, and I also did not see any wings. In addition, I did not hear the angel talk. We communicated totally through telepathy.

According to the book of Revelation, some of the living creatures that are around God's throne also have faces as animals and men. They also have wings. Another thought is that cobras seem to have played a major role in some of the dynasties in Egypt. Again, can we assume that these fallen angels may have shared something that they saw in heaven with the Egyptians? Is it hard on the imagination to think of Satan as a cobra or having something to do with the cobra? He was a serpent, and the cobra seems to have been venerated in the culture of one of the first great empires. I am sure that there are many books on this subject, but I wanted to share my thoughts with you.

Now, it is not so difficult for one to see that the gods of Egypt may not have been just someone's imagination. The cobra may have been chosen as a symbol for a reason that seemed logical at the time. As stated, many of you have seen it on the golden mask of King Tut. With Satan and his demons here on earth, they could influence men and probably had a great amount of influence before the church came onto the scene. These gods of Egypt may be a realistic portrait of an influence that these angels had on the people.

These fallen angels came from heaven. They knew things about heaven that the people who lived on earth did not know. They had an advanced knowledge about mechanics, space, and times. Even Job, whose book is considered to be the oldest book in the Bible, knew that earth was set in the heavens upon nothing. Only someone with a vast amount of knowledge from someone who was celestial or terrestrial at that time would have known that. Or he could have seen visions that came from God. At any rate, I truly believe that most humans know that something is going on in the supernatural that can't be totally explained at this time.

On the other hand, we have the Bible and the words of the prophets. Many people seek knowledge, but most never find it because they are not looking in the right place. According to 2 Corinthians 4:3, if the gospel is hidden, it is hidden to the persons that are lost. That is a powerful statement. For those of you who are lost and don't believe what I have written, or who don't believe the Bible, please take a moment to search yourself before it is too late. Is it too hard to believe the Bible, or to believe me, since I am a mere mortal? Please try not to be critical of the Bible or of me until you have searched and found answers for yourself. Do your own research, and then present your questions.

The Bible states that Satan is the god or power over this world. Even Jesus calls Satan the prince of this world. Paul in 2 Corinthians 4:4 also states that Satan is the god of this world and that he blinds the minds of those who do not believe that Jesus Christ is our Lord and Savior.

Again, if the gospel is hidden, it is hidden from those who are lost. Since Satan is the prince of this world, I am sure he has his hands in a number of things that go on down here. Most people that I have met believe in evil and believe that people can do evil deeds to hurt each other. I pose a question to you: If God is higher and mightier than Satan, why don't most people believe in His miracle-working powers? Is it hard to believe that God hears and answers prayers? Is it difficult to believe in His power? Please do your own research before it is too late.

I found it exciting to note the discussion in *Prophecy in the News* magazine (Dr. J. R. Church and Gary Stearman, "The Ancient Book of Enoch," *Prophecy in the News*, February 2009, 35). Dr. J. R. Church discusses the book of Enoch and fallen angels. According to Dr. Church, "Semjâzâ was the leader of (a group or the group) of angels who fell. The fallen angels mated with women on earth and taught them things that were prohibited by God. In the book of Enoch, chapter 8:1: Azâzêl taught mankind to make swords and knives and shields and coats of mail, and taught them to see what was behind them, and their works of art; bracelets and ornaments, and the use of rouge, and the beautifying of the eyebrows (most of us have noticed the dark eye liner on Egyptian paintings and artifacts, and King Tut's mask. Also, the heavy makeup and paint for the face in other cultures), and the dearest and choicest stones and all coloring substances and the metals of the earth. Chapter 8:2: And there was great wickedness and much fornication, and they sinned, and all their ways were corrupt. Chapter 8:3: Amêzârâk taught all the conjurers and root-cutters, Armârôs taught the loosening of conjurations; Baraq'âl the astrologers, Kôkâbêl the signs, and Temêl taught astrology, and Asrâdêl taught the course of the moon."

According to passages in the book of Enoch above, I believe that this sums up the fact that Satan and his angels helped to lead mankind into a number of sins that did not please God. I must say that I never knew that the names of the fallen angels were listed in a book. After sharing this fact with a number of people, it appears that some aren't aware of this either. I found this information to be extremely interesting, and plan to purchase Dr. J. R. Church's book on Enoch in the future.

Before I go any further, on May 17, 2016, I was working on this manuscript around 4:00 a.m. My daughter came into the room, and she stated that she had a strange dream. She was told in a vision to call "him" by his name. She tried to pronounce a name that was very similar to Azazel. She was pronouncing a name that started with an A, but it ended in "isis." I really don't know what this means at this time.

A last note on the UFO phenomenon is the fact that I would like to note here that I have read and heard that a number of astronauts have made statements about UFO encounters. Also, some countries started opening their files on UFOs in 2010. This history of UFOs has been very secretive, until now. What are UFOs? I strongly believe that they are vehicles for the fallen angels and their demons to move around. I also believe that aliens are the fallen angels or their demons. Today, a number of people are coming forward to discuss the UFO phenomenon. There is a history on the web about this subject with the dates, places, and people who encountered these spaceships. You may want to look it up on the web.

Could someone else have been there on the moon with our spacecrafts when they landed? It is a possibility. Look it up for yourself, and you decide. Also, I remember my family having a conversation about it sometime in years past. It was a scary time for us as I look back because we were in the dark about the first flight to the moon. I remember people having conversations in the neighborhood stating that the flight to the moon never happened. It was all a hoax to them. In addition, I remember looking at the evening news during the Discovery flight in 1991. There was an interesting news flash on the television that day. My family, friends, and I saw what the news anchor, I don't remember which channel I was on, described as (maybe) a battle between two UFOs in space. Was it real? I don't know, but it certainly looked real. It was aired several times during the day, but I've only seen it one other time on the television. You may, however, look it up on the web.

My Third Vision of the Rapture with a Day

Around the middle of October 2007, I had another vision of the Rapture. It was late in the evening; twilight. Please know that twilight can be early evening or early morning. I was cooking eggs in a frying pan. Although it was dusk outside, and I was cooking eggs, it did not feel like the morning. It really felt like the twilight of the evening, just before the sun sets. I could hear the shofar blow, loud and long with purpose. I spoke immediately without hesitation, "I didn't think that the Rapture would occur on a Monday." I then walked to the door and looked out. I could see people raptured as if they were starburst against the evening sky. Again, I did not see that many people raptured. I heard the shofar this time, but I woke up before I could go any further in the vision. Additionally, I did not feel any impending danger of any sort before the shofar was blown, because I was in the kitchen with the door open. I want to make this very clear: I was given a day for the Rapture, not an actual date. However, the angel did not appear to me again. It was me who said this. Please remember that Satan is the Lord of this world. Did he try to duplicate the Rapture for me in this manner? Does this explain the day/night conundrum? I don't know. I just had to put this note about Satan in the manuscript. Please note:

On April 27, 2009, my daughter came into my bedroom with a smile on her face. She said the Lord told her, "Tell your mom that she is correct about Monday." My daughter stated she had a vision that the Lord told her to tell me this because I was hesitant about telling people that the Rapture would happen on this day. My daughter stated that the Lord appeared to her and told her this statement and to let me know. He then placed her in front of me in the vision, so that she could tell me at that moment. When she awoke, she immediately came to my room and told me that I was correct about the day.

I can now say that I have witnessed two very distinct visions of the Rapture, and a vision of UFOs lined up in formation, which led me to relate it to the Rapture. The first vision was during the day. The sky was a deep blue with two small snowy white clouds placed to the left of the entrance of the planet and angel. During the first vision, I could not hear the shofar; nor was I raptured. I saw people who were raptured as first shrinking down until they could not be seen anymore and disappearing in the twinkling of an eye. Their clothing was taken with them and was not left in heaps on the ground. During the second vision, I could hear the shofar and see people raptured as if they were starbursts in the sky. Lastly, during the third vision, I saw the UFOs in what I believed was a military formation.

Now, this presents to me a question: "How long does the Rapture go on?" This has got to be one of the questions to be answered after seeing the two distinct visions, or is it? The Rapture may take as long as a day to occur, since one vision was definitely during the day and the other vision was at twilight. I don't like to guess with the Lord or with prophecy, but this may be the answer.

For years, I have understood that the Bible states that of "that day" and hour, no man will know. This is what I've been taught, and it is in the Bible several times. However, I don't know if this statement is about the Rapture or the Day of the Lord. Therefore, I prayed for several months and asked the Lord why I had been given a day. The answer came to me one day when I got ready for my praise and worship service here at the house. I went to my Bible and turned to Matthew 24:42, which states that "for ye know not what hour your Lord doth come."

> *"Watch therefore: for ye know not what hour your Lord doth come.*
>
> *"But know this, that if the goodman of the house had known in what watch the thief would come, he would have watched, and would not have suffered his house to be broken up.*
>
> *"Therefore be ye also ready: for in such an hour as ye think not the Son of man cometh" (Matthew 24:42–44).*

I was taken aback when I saw this! The word "day" of the Lord's return is not written in verse 42. It only states that you will not know the hour when the Lord doth come. The verses above talk about the goodman of the house. If the goodman had known in what watch the thief would come, he would have watched, and would not have suffered his house to be broken up. In addition, the Bible states that the Day of the Lord will come as a thief in the night, according to 1 Thessalonians 5:2. I have heard this chapter and verse preached as "judgment" and "the Second Coming of Jesus after the tribulation." I don't know, but I believe I was guided to it. Please study for yourselves because I don't have the answer from the Lord at this time.

Additionally, I also may have seen the Day of the Lord that seems to come after the Rapture. However, I am not sure, and the Lord has not made this clear for me yet. Let's just think for a moment. The Rapture may be an event that will last for several hours. I did not see cars wrecking, planes falling from the sky, or trains crashing on the tracks. It may have occurred, but I did not see it. I was too overwhelmed by the people plundering homes in my neighborhood. I also must note that I was confined to a small area of my city. It may have happened, but I don't know.

At any rate, I continue to have a problem stating anything that I'm not sure of at this time. Jesus stated in Matthew 24:36 that no man or angel knows of the day and hour for His coming, not even the angels in heaven. Father God is the only one who knows the day and the hour for the Day of the Lord. However, for me, the Day of the Lord appears to be different from the Rapture. Father God, please forgive me if I am wrong.

The Rapture, Day of the Lord, and the tribulation appear to be three separate events. After the Rapture, there may be several years before the tribulation starts. Although, it appeared that the tribulation occurred after the Rapture, with people running wild in the streets. It also appears that the tribulation starts after the Abomination of Desolation in Matthew 5:21. If that is true, I believe I have enough information that states the saints will be gone when the Antichrist is revealed. It is the Antichrist who commits the Abomination of Desolation, and he who letteth will let until he be taken away. I think the saints are gone before the great tribulation begins. We have tribulation now, but Jesus states that the great tribulation will be worse than any since the beginning of the world. People, do you understand? It will be worse than the destructions of Jerusalem, Sodom and Gomorrah, Babylon, Rome, or Egypt. Father God, help us.

God loves us. I believe that, just as we are given a warning that that glorious and great day is at hand (even now, people). God will prepare the world for this event. He is doing it now, and most of you are not listening. We also may have time to stop the cars, planes, trains, and other means of transportation, since I did not see them wreck. Another thought is that it will stop automatically because I had to walk to find my family members as mentioned earlier. I must say, I don't know. Again, I only felt danger after the Rapture occurred in my first vision. However, things happened very quickly. After I talked to the angel, time seemed to have escalated. It appeared that many hours had passed from the time of the Rapture to the time that the angel disappeared. When my attention and thoughts came back to earth, there was total mayhem here.

Lastly, please remember that I stated in the present tense, "I didn't think that the Rapture would occur on a Monday." Another thought is this: Israel is God's time line for prophecy. We have several hours during the day when it is daylight there and night time here in America. I may have experienced the day/night timeline here on earth. I really don't know the answer; just be ready when He comes. Where are you going?

A VISION AND
COUNTERFEIT VISION

*"Call unto me, and I will answer thee, and show thee great
and mighty things, which thou knowest not" (Jeremiah 33:3).*

The Lord has shown me great and mighty things. Let me state something interesting here. My family started noting that we would awaken at 3:33 a.m., and during the day, we would walk by the clock at exactly 3:33 p.m. This continued for several weeks in 2011. Needless to say, we were confounded. One day, we were talking with my siblings and their families and realized that they also were experiencing the same thing. All of us had been noticing this phenomenon and had not mentioned it to the others. Nevertheless, we didn't know what to make of this time conundrum. Anyway, we prayed about it and continued to watch certain shows on the Christian television channels. After praying and listening to evangelists on television having the same experience with the number 333 or the time 3:33, we were led to Jeremiah 33:3. Please note it above. The Lord wants us to call unto Him, and He will answer and show us great and mighty things. Isn't this exciting? Again, a number of us are seeing the same things. Strength comes in numbers, and this certainly boosted my confidence. I also tried in vain to get a message to some of these evangelists to note their experience with this time miracle. I know these men and women of God are busy, but I tried.

Let me add an interesting note here. Not too long after this revelation, the number 333 came out in the Pick 3 state lotto game. My family and I made note of it because we were dealing with this number in the manner that I mentioned above. Anyway, I had a vision during the night after this number came out. I saw myself entering the corner store. Someone met me at the door and said, "Play the number 555 for the Pick 3 tonight." I said, "Why should I play that number, when 333 just came out? The odds are against me." The person's face was shrouded, and I could not see who was talking. I could, however, see a hand with the number 555 written on a piece of paper. While in the vision, this voice continued to insist that I play the number 555, and I continued to resist. Nevertheless, when I woke up that next day, I told everyone that I had a message to play the number 555 even though I could not see who was talking. Well, I went to the corner store and bought several of the Pick 3 numbers. And they were indeed the number 555. I will emphasize again that I did not see who was telling me to play the number 555, but I played it anyway, although I had resisted this person in the vision. As you probably know by now, I did not win. Therefore, it is very safe to state that all visions that occur without a known messenger from the Lord can't be trusted. Remember—I did not see who was speaking to me. I learned the hard way by losing money on that Pick 3. On another note, I had a vision of my son telling me that a ticket would cost him $1,679. I played that number for fun, and it did, indeed, come out, but not in that order.

Even though people are witnesses to the Rapture, some remain ignorant of the fact that the Rapture is taking place. Instead of repenting and finding favor in the Lord to go up, there will be murders, thefts, fornication, and sorceries. Look at Revelation 9:20–21, which states that men will continue to worship devils, idols of gold and silver, and brass, and stone, and wood. People, do you know that these items cannot see, hear, or walk? Why worship them? On another note, some people will look to black magic and sorcery. Satan is coming, and his name is Antichrist. He can't help you. He can only condemn your souls to hell. Where are you going?

> *"And the rest of the men which were not killed by these plagues yet repented not of the works of their hands, that they should not worship devils, and idols of gold, and silver, and brass, and stone, and of wood: which neither can see, nor hear, nor walk" (Revelation 9:20).*

Instead of bowing to the Lord God, many people will continue to make allegiances to their idols during these days of tribulation. They believe in their devils and images that were made by hand. Some of these statues have been placed in churches and temples that are made by hand and are symbolic of their Gods. These statues, idols, and devils can't work any miracles for you: they were never able to work miracles. Repent before it is too late. Why do so many people believe that images made by the hands of men, here on earth, can actually govern their lives? Read your Bibles and believe. You are not gods, and you can't make a god with your hands. These images can't see, hear, or talk. There is an image that the Antichrist will make after the church is raptured, and it will do some of these things. You may read about this in the book of Revelation.

On another note, once twilight has passed, what comes next? Darkness comes after the twilight of evening. During the day, I saw firsthand that people were evil and were committing two (theft and murder) of the many things that Revelation 9:20–21 states that they will continue to do, even after the Rapture. I saw people running wild without showing any regard for each other or respect for anyone's possessions in their homes. These people will overrun your houses. Imagine, if you will, when the night has always been a favorite covering for acts of evil, how frightening this day will become.

Jesus died for our sins to be forgiven so that we, who believe, may be delivered up to be with Him when He comes. If He did not die for our sins and ascend on the third day, why would His disciples and apostles go to the trouble of writing a record of Him? These men had to see and know for sure that these acts did take place. They were witnesses to the Son of God's many miracles that He performed here on earth.

How many of you have had a stroke of luck and said, "Thank you, Lord."? Do you continue to praise Him and thank Him? I think not, until you have near catastrophes and scream, "The Lord saved me!" Nevertheless, do you think to commune with Him continuously? The Lord wants to hear you pray and try Him. Just "try" Him, and ask Him for what you want before it is too late.

WHY DREAMS AND VISIONS

"And he said, Hear now my words: If there be a prophet among you, I the LORD will make myself known unto him in a vision, and will speak unto him in a dream" (Numbers 12:6).

"Now a thing was secretly brought to me, and mine ear received a little thereof.

"In thoughts from the visions of the night, when deep sleep falleth on men,

"Fear came upon me, and trembling, which made all my bones to shake.

"Then a spirit passed before my face; the hair of my flesh stood up. (Job 4:12–15).

"Then thou scarest me with dreams, and terrifiest me through visions" (Job 7:14).

"I Daniel was grieved in my spirit in the midst of my body, and the visions of my head troubled me" (Daniel 7:15).

Again, visions and dreams are a way for the Lord to communicate with us. Visions and dreams can be very frightening and scary, as stated in the books of Job and Daniel. I responded to the dreams and visions in the same manner as the people in these verses state. Eliphaz the Temanite is speaking in Job 4:12–15. He was terrified by visions of the night. Job's thoughts are in Job 7:14. He was scared of his dreams and terrified of the visions that he saw. Daniel's thoughts are in Daniel 7:15. Note how Daniel was grieved when he saw the dreams and visions that the Lord sent to him. It may be noted that Daniel fainted at one point because of the visions. I, myself, literally stopped praying for a while because I was seeing so much, and I was very afraid. I am not comparing myself to these people in the Bible, but we reacted in similar manners after seeing these visions. All of you should be aware that some visions are horrific. They can be extremely frightening. This is my purpose for adding the above verses, for you to know that I wasn't the only one who was afraid.

One night, after I had gotten into bed and closed my eyes, I immediately heard the sound of wings flapping in my room. I was scared to no end. I kept my eyes closed and asked Father God to take it away. The sound left immediately. I felt empty after this happened, and I have not heard this sound again. We are, however, not to be fearful. Yet, I was too frightened to open my eyes and face what was in front of me. Now, I feel empty and hope that I hear this sound again. I want to know what it was. I should also note that it took almost two years from this occurrence for me to see more visions after I sent this one away.

According to Daniel 4:13, he saw a watcher and a holy one come down from heaven. Are the watchers the demons? Are the holy ones angels? Regardless of who they are, we are being watched. I believe that the wings that I heard flapping were those of angels.

One needs to consider why we have dreams and visions. One reason is for the Lord God to talk to us. Another is for angels of the Lord to bring us messages. And why does the Lord talk to us and send us messages? He and His angels see and hear us. Again, we are watched.

Dreams and visions can be frightening, but consider, if you will, the terms "watcher" and "holy one" first. Have you ever thought or felt as though you were being watched? Or have you ever caught a shadow from the corner of your eye, or just felt that you were not alone? The angel that I saw knew everything that I felt and thought. I felt as though I was being put on notice because of the things that I was thinking in my head. Now that I know that my actions and yours are being observed, I am extremely aware of my actions and my attitude. For the angel to know me and what was in my head and heart proves that someone is indeed watching! Is anyone listening? Your very thoughts are being recorded along with your actions.

Get your Bible and read it. Pray and ask for understanding before you read. Ask Father God for protection from Satan when you pray because he intensifies his attacks when you pray. You may have dreams and visions, but don't be afraid. I cannot overemphasize how frightening these visions and dreams can be. Believe me. Satan is also watching, for he also walks the earth. He seeks the righteous and tries to destroy them just as he did Job. Our faith should be as strong as Job's, so that we can overcome Satan's attacks.

The book of Daniel and his reference to the watchers has always fascinated me. I often wonder if we have someone in heaven who was assigned the job of being a watcher for us. Do they see everything that we do? I pray now that my sins will not find me. I have prayed for forgiveness for my sins, and I have accepted my Lord and Savior Jesus Christ in the free pardon of my sins. I now solicit you to do the same, for the hour is very near for the Rapture. If the things that you are doing don't feel right and holy to do, then, don't do them. I look at earth as though it is the final showplace, or the last stop, on our way to salvation. Yes, you are being watched, and you are being put to the test. Each and every one of us is in dire need of reassessing our soul's appointment. If the things that you are doing don't line up with the Bible, stop them now!

Oftentimes when we see things that are out of the norm, we become afraid and fearful. I was too afraid to write the visions when I first saw them. Again, according to Habakkuk 2:2, the Lord demands that we write down the visions that we see. I now know why that is the case; as I read this information, I try to recall the visions as they were. This is not possible for all of them. There are some things that I have forgotten, and I dare not try to speculate. The Lord demands that we write the vision and make it plain. Why would He instruct us to write a vision down if it did not mean anything? These visions have meaning.

After seeing the vision of the Rapture, I started to speculate as to whether or not I saw an angel or the Lord Himself. The person that I saw was as an enormous man who filled the sky! He had dark hair with a little gray on the sides. His hair came down to the nape of his neck, and he appeared to have a small band or braid around his forehead to hold his hair in place. I don't want to get too much into his physical description, because I don't want my readers to focus on the bearer instead of the message. However, here is some information. The person that I saw did not have wings that I could see. He wore a light or white linen garment that covered his feet and was bound at his waist. We communicated without speaking to one another. We spoke by telepathy; he knew what I was feeling and thinking, and I, in turn, knew what he was saying without us verbalizing anything to one another. There are many descriptions of angels in the Bible and the living creatures that are heavenly, but I saw a man. He did not tell me his name; therefore, I started saying that I saw an angel of the Lord. As I saw more visions and began to read more, I believe that I may have seen the Lord Jesus Christ. Nevertheless, I must stress that, at this time, I do not know who I saw.

An added note made on March 6, 2010, at 11:27 p.m.: I can definitely state that I saw an angel of the Lord because I saw a vision of Jesus Christ since the above statement was written and knew that I had seen Him. I don't want to take away any material, but add to what I have already written. Since the visions continue to come, I, in turn, will continue to add information.

> *"He cast upon them the fierceness of his anger, wrath, and indignation, and trouble, by sending evil angels among them.*
> *"He made a way to his anger; he spared not their soul from death, but gave their life over to the pestilence"* (Psalm 78:49–50).

We all know that there are angels in heaven and fallen angels that are here on earth. Please be aware of this fact: the patience of God is continuous. God punishes all of the people He loves. We all go through trials and tribulations, but it is a wise person who learns his lesson and repents from his sins. Do not tempt the Lord with disobedience, for He can send plagues. God also will send evil angels among us. Most Christians know that there are good angels and evil angels. Do they look different? Yes, they do. I know from my visions when I am in the presence of good and evil most of the time. I know that I have been around people, too, who appear to be the embodiment of evil. Have you felt the same way? Maybe I was dealing with an evil angel or agent of Satan.

Note: again, I have been reading a commentary on the ancient book of Enoch that Dr. J. R. Church has been discussing in his monthly magazine. (Dr. J. R. Church and Gary Stearman, *Prophecy in the News*, 2009). If evil angels can be sent to earth, this may be an explanation as to why some people are so wicked. However, I believe that evil people have no idea as to their fate. They become absorbed in the lusts and cares of the world and forget where their rewards are after death.

According to Dr. J. R. Church, in his monthly magazine, (Dr. J. R. Church and Gary Stearman, "The Ancient Book of Enoch," *Prophecy in the News*, March 2009, 38), when evil people die, "but as to the unjust, they are dragged by force to the left hand by the angels allotted for punishment, no longer going with a good-will, but as prisoners driven by violence; to whom are sent the angels appointed over them to reproach them and threaten them with their terrible looks and to thrust them still downwards. No [sic] those angels that are set over these should, drag them into the neighborhood of hell itself; who, when they are hard by it, continually hear the noise of it, and do not stand clear of the hot vapor itself; terrible and exceeding great prospect of fire, they are struck with a fearful expectation of a future judgment, and in effect punished thereby; and not only so, but where they see the place of the fathers of the just, even hereby are they punished; for a chaos deep and large is fixed between them; insomuch that a just man that hath compassion upon them cannot be admitted, nor can one that is unjust if he were bold enough to attempt it, pass over it" (*Josephus's Discourse to the Greeks concerning Hades*, paragraphs 3 and 4).

This appears to be a description of the place that the rich man and Lazarus were held until Jesus Christ delivered His saints to paradise after His death and resurrection. We will discuss this later. However, the angels in charge of Hades or hell will actually drag the soul of the unrighteous to this place after the unjust person dies. These evil angels are set over these souls that become prisoners, who are driven by violence. These particular angels are terrible or scary in appearance. Is this the place that all of you unrighteous people are knocking down the door to get to? Imagine dying, and the next thing that you notice are these angels dragging your souls to Hades. Just the thought of having these horrible-looking angels dragging your souls down to Hades should make you pause and think about your actions while you are alive and can repent. I don't believe anyone wants his or her soul to be destined to a place such as this. I think most people have forgotten that Hades, or hell, is real, and evil people are destined to go there. Where are you going?

Satan is in the business of tempting people here on earth. The story of Job is very important because it is a testament to the faith that one has in God to avoid the fiery pits of hell. Satan petitioned God to let him test the faith of Job. God trusted in the faith of Job and allowed Satan to challenge Job with many tragedies. However, Job endured and was given more in the end than he had before Satan attempted to destroy his faith. Does God give men on earth over to Satan to test their faith today? I think He does and, remember, Christians are long-suffering. This is just my thought because my family and I have had many trials. I, too, feel like Job.

The world is suffering at this time. There are whispers among the people of the world that God is sending some kind of judgment on us. A number of catastrophes are happening that man can't explain. A majority of the world's population is suffering some type of crisis. I believe that we are witnessing the fierceness of God's anger because we do not honor Him and His commandments. We need to repent and bow down on our knees and pray. We don't need to be dragged to hell when we can go to heaven.

THE DREAM THAT KEPT ON GOING

This next vision was very puzzling, to say the least. I can only state that it was strange. I lay in my bed beside my husband on December 1, 2007, and had a dream or vision like none that I can explain. If it was a dream, it did not end but kept going. If it was a vision, I was taken full circle. This is how it happened:

Inside of the dream or vision, one of my sisters had found a house that she liked and wanted to purchase. My sister and I found ourselves in the dream standing together in front of the house, which appeared to be a castle. It was huge and had turrets or towers on two corners of the house.

The telephone rang in my bedroom and woke me up. I answered it and went back to sleep.

I found myself back in the dream. In the dream, my sister was now inside the house signing papers and saying that she wanted this house. Two women were there with her, encouraging her to sign some papers. I went inside and grabbed the papers and told my sister that she was not signing anything until we looked around the house. One girl tried to take the papers away from me. I told her that I would beat her up if she tried to get these papers from me. I must state that I don't know what this means.

The telephone rang in my bedroom and woke me up. I answered it and went back to sleep.

I found myself back in the dream. In the dream, my sister and I were now in the master bedroom of the house. My sister never spoke. I seemed to have done all of the talking. I said that the room was big and nice and that I liked it very much because of the room's expanse.

The telephone rang in my bedroom and woke me up. I answered it and went back to sleep.

I found myself back in the dream. In the dream, my sister and I were now in a pretty pink girl's room. The room was nice and big. However, it was narrow, and quite long. I told my sister that I liked the room, but it was too far away from the master bedroom and that she could not keep an eye on the children. This was strange because my sister's children are adults.

The telephone rang in my bedroom and woke me up. I answered it and went back to sleep.

I went back in the dream. In the dream, my sister and I found ourselves in a large family room that was very nice and airy. The kitchen was next to this room.

The telephone rang in my bedroom and woke me up. I answered it and went back to sleep.

I found myself back in the dream. In the dream, my sister and I were now looking over the kitchen. I said to her that it was really nice and big but that I wanted to see the back of the house.

The telephone rang in my bedroom and woke me up. I answered it and went back to sleep.

I found myself back in the dream. In the dream, my sister and I were now standing on the back of the house. We could only see half of it. It appeared to have a sunken back with only the top floor showing. A calming little brook ran down behind the house, and I could see the rooftops of several other houses in the distance. I told my sister that I really liked this house.

The telephone rang in my bedroom and woke me up. I answered it and went back to sleep.

I found myself back in the dream. In the dream, my sister and I found ourselves back in the kitchen. I told her that I liked the house and that I needed to get my daughter and leave. My daughter suddenly appeared from a corner of the room. She was much younger, and I was startled when I saw her, but I don't know why. Then, I woke up and sat up in the bed.

I have no idea what this dream or vision was about. Neither have I been given a reason or an answer to it at this time. It was so real and unusual that I feel that there is a meaning that may be revealed later. Added note: I received an answer about this dream on November 13, 2014. It was a warning for my daughter.

I have experienced recurring dreams in the past with me at my grandmother's old home or my mom and dad's old home, but never a dream like this one that goes on and on. One might ask also about the number of times that the telephone rang. I come from a large family, and we may call each other two or three times a day. I also continue to have trouble trying to come to some logical explanation as to why I was so upset with my sister for attempting to sign the papers for the house. This was very strange indeed.

In the past, I have dreamed about our parents' last home. It was unique and had an L-shaped porch. The dream started with me looking at the house from the outside, and it looked like our normal old home. Every four months or so, I would dream that I was inside of the house, and with each dream the house became an enormous mansion. I started out in the living room and continued to go farther into the house with each vision. The last and final vision, to date, came several years ago when I finally reached the attic and found a man and his son making handbags. I have never dreamed about this house again. I think that the message was about the economy with the handbags as a clue, maybe. Or it may be the fact that my financial situation was about to change. This vision may have been a warning, since hints of an economic failure preceded my first vision of the Rapture.

People, this is it. The end of this life, as we know it, is very near. The Rapture can occur at any time, and the sad news is, not too many people are going. You are not ready. Please read and study the Bible. You need to know what is expected of you as a Christian.

> "And grieve not the holy Spirit of God, whereby ye are sealed unto the day of redemption.
> "Let all bitterness, and wrath, and anger, and clamour, and evil speaking, be put away from you, with all malice.
> "And be ye kind one to another, tenderhearted, forgiving one another, even as God for Christ's sake hath forgiven you" (Ephesians 4:30–32).

I had been dealing with unforgivingness in my heart before I saw the vision of the Rapture. I guess one could say that I was grieving the

Holy Spirit as noted in verse 30 above. I was unrepentant in the grief that grasped my emotions and caused me to spend most of my waking moments on trying to figure out why I was feeling the pain that I was feeling. I felt that I was owed an explanation as to why some things were happening in my life that caused me a great amount of pain. I had to remember that we are to be meek with long-suffering and forbearing one another in love.

For believing Christians, the Holy Spirit lives within us. Our bodies become the earthly domain for the Holy Spirit when we believe and accept Jesus Christ as our Lord and Savior. The Holy Spirit compels us to live, walk, talk, and carry ourselves in a godly manner. We can grieve the Holy Spirit when we act contrary to the Christian lifestyle. This is what I was doing. I felt as though my family and I had been mistreated, and I was waiting around for someone to apologize for the hurt and pain that they were causing. Let me strongly emphasize this again. I felt that I had been mistreated, and still do, as a matter of fact. But it was my responsibility, as a Christian, to go to the people who had mistreated me! Although the people that I had to go to and express these feelings did not acknowledge the sincerity of the message, I obeyed my Father and took the message directly to them. I did not wait another day. When I saw the vision of the Rapture and did not go up, I was told that it was I who had to go to those people and tell them that I forgive them and that I love them. I went that day to each person's home because I was afraid of being left behind down here on earth. I did not want to go through the horrors of what I saw happening here on earth after the Rapture. And most importantly, I felt better. I felt as if a weight had been lifted off of my heart and that I was now ready to go up whenever God called. It was so amazing that those simple words, "I forgive you, and I love you," were the words that kept me in this turmoil that was here on earth because I lacked them in my heart. Think about it, if you will. Are there any people who have wronged you and against whom you are holding grudges? Let it go. Do not grieve any longer, and let the Holy Spirit live within you in peace. Believe me; you do not want to be left down here. My message is simple and matter-of-fact: forgive and love everyone. It is so simple when you consider the matter. Do you want to be left here because you can't forgive and love? All Christians in Christ know that this is what you need to do.

It is also interesting to note that there are watchers and holy ones watching us. We are on a stage or the other side of the veil, and everything that we think, say, and do is being recorded. How did the angel know what I was feeling? He knew, and it is recorded somewhere. He let me know that he knew everything that I was feeling. He also knew that it was too late for me to change once the shofar had been blown. Too many people are in danger of it "being too late" for them also.

It is evident from reading the Bible that spirits need a body to live in on earth. The Holy Spirit lives in the body of believing Christians, and the body can also be an earthly domain for evil spirits. If the Holy Spirit does abide in us, He cleanses and empowers us to live a Christian life. Also, He will cause unclean spirits to leave. Please note:

> *"When the unclean spirit is gone out of a man, he walketh through dry places, seeking rest; and finding none, he saith, I will return unto my house whence I came out.*
> *"And when he cometh, he findeth it swept and garnished.*
> *"Then goeth he, and taketh to him seven other spirits more wicked than himself; and they enter in, and dwell there: and the last state of that man is worse than the first"* (Luke 11:24–26).

Please notice that an unclean (evil spirit) can inhabit an earthly body too. They are territorial and call bodies here on earth their home. I believe that spirits need bodies to survive on earth. Verse 24 states that the unclean spirit can go away from earthly bodies. I believe this means that people, here on earth, can be delivered from an unclean spirit. People can be delivered from unclean spirits by accepting the Lord Jesus Christ and His commandments. When people do not accept the Lord Jesus, these unclean spirits can find a home in a body that does not have the Holy Spirit living there. The Holy Spirit and living a Christian life will make the body clean and cause an unclean spirit to leave. However, the unclean spirit can come back. I think these spirits can and do come back when we, Christians, spiral into unforgivingness, lead lives that are not pleasing to God, or become backsliding Christians who are doing things that we know are wrong. When this unclean spirit comes back and finds that the body that it left has been cleaned, it (unclean spirit) brings seven unclean spirits that are more wicked than itself, and the last state of a person's body is worse than the first. Do you know people who are like this? They are people who seem daily to grow more wicked.

I would like to give a personal experience here through which the Lord helped me. I went to a local store two weeks from the writing of this message. I parked my car and left an empty space beside me and the next car to avoid getting dents and dings from the next car. A woman drove up beside me into that empty space. I heard her passenger telling her to go up to the next space and leave the space empty beside me. The woman ignored her passenger and parked beside me anyway. The woman's passenger kept telling her that she was wrong to do that. I thought, oh well, and I got out of my car and went into the store. When I got back to my car, I noticed a brown stain that was smeared on my back passenger window. It looked like snuff (most southerners know what this is) or human excrement, since the woman had small children in the car. I was incensed with anger and sat down in my car trying to decide how to get this woman back. First, I wanted revenge, and I wanted it then. I looked around the parking lot and noticed a woman on a cell phone, parked in front of this woman's car. I sat there scheming how to get revenge. I was going to get something/ anything and smear it onto this woman's car. However, the woman on the cell phone would not move. I sat there for two minutes and contemplated evil because I was mad. Added note to my brothers and sisters: we are not mad animals. We are loving Christians. Anyway, a calming spirit came over me. The Lord explained in my spirit that this woman was embodied with evil. He told me that I was dealing with the devil incarnate. Can any of you see how easily we Christians can be distracted and offended? I wanted revenge and sat there scheming how to get it, but the Lord calmed me down and let me know with whom I was dealing. All of a sudden, this matter became trivial and reminded me of the evil that was living in this woman. I felt sorry for her, and told the Lord to handle the situation for me. People, you need to be careful of the things that you do out of malice to God's children. I explain it like this: when God spanks you, it hurts. I knew that I had not done anything to this woman for her to behave badly, but the Lord knew what was in her heart. As a matter of fact, I didn't know her. Again, we Christians are to love and forgive. It is very difficult at times. Even so, I started my car and drove off as I prayed to the Lord for this woman and gave her over to Him.

> *"Arise, O LORD; save me, O my God: for thou hast smitten all mine enemies upon the cheek bone; thou hast broken the teeth of the ungodly" (Psalm 3:7).*

The Lord will smite our enemies on the cheek and break their teeth. We don't have to seek revenge. Leave it to the Lord and live holy lives. This woman may be suffering and doesn't know why, but I do. Here is a little humor: Do you know of someone who has done you wrong and that person is missing some teeth? God may have sought revenge for you in His way. People, remember that the Lord will seek revenge for you instead of you getting angry and opening up doors for Satan and his demons to come into your heart by filling it with vengeance. Keep revenge out of your heart. The Lord will hit your enemies in the jaw and break their teeth. I must give credit to Dr. J. R. Church and Gary Stearman of *Prophecy in the News* for mentioning Psalm 3:7 on their television program. Dr. Church mentioned this bit of humor on a show. Anyway, I think this statement is very appropriate for this woman.

Earth after the Rapture

The time that followed after the Rapture occurred was full of violence and mayhem on an unthinkable level. The economy was in shambles, and danger was all around. No one was safe. Some Christians who knew of the saving grace of our Lord and Savior Jesus Christ were sad to realize that if they had possessed love and forgiveness, they would have been taken up to meet the Lord in the Rapture. It seemed so easy to love and forgive people now that it was too late. How many of you reading this book are holding in bad thoughts against someone and do not know how to love anymore or how to forgive? On the other hand, people who were evil and who did not know our Lord and Savior Jesus Christ were worse than before the Rapture. I saw evil prevailing at every turn. People were killing for any object of safety that one was holding; it could have been a gun, a knife, or a metal pipe. Anything that one could use as a weapon for defense was reason to be killed so that someone else could possess that weapon. To me, it seemed as though most of the people who were left were the embodiment of evil, and it appeared to me as though I was dealing with Satan face to face with every stranger that I encountered.

The Lord has placed it upon my heart to show all who read this book that He is coming soon. It takes a moment to love and forgive anyone who has harmed you. Do it now. It will be much too late to do it when the angel appears with the shofar and blows it, but you can't hear a sound, because you can't go up in the Rapture. It will be too late to realize that holding grief and unforgivingness in our hearts can cause a lifetime of pain and suffering for those who are left behind.

Let me repeat again: I also saw the world that will be left here after the Rapture occurs. The world will be filled with violence on a scale that no one has seen before. Immediately after the Rapture took place, I saw people looking for weapons of any kind to defend themselves. And if you were fortunate enough to have even a stick, you would be killed in the street, and that stick would be taken away from you. It is going to be a horrible sight to see your loved ones beaten and killed in the streets because people will not be fully aware of what is happening. Yes, I said that you and your loved ones will be killed in the streets by lawless, Satan-driven madness and pandemonium on a global scale. As it is true for most people of today, most of you don't believe in my God, the God of Abraham, Isaac, and Jacob, or in the Rapture. I am here to tell you, my friend, that it is all so real.

Imagine if you will a Hurricane Katrina or the tsunami of 2004 happening all at once, worldwide. No, not the actual forces of nature, but the horrors that the people who survived them had to endure. Everyone can remember the horrors that the people had to endure during Katrina. This is the type of horror that will occur all over the world. Now imagine acts of self-preservation on a worldwide scale ballooning into unspeakable acts of savagery and mayhem. Lawlessness will abound. What about your loved ones? How will you know who was raptured and who was left? Can you imagine the horrors of trying to get through a city or state or another country while trying to find your loved ones? Believe me, all I saw was violence, and no one had a plan for the ones who will be left here. Is the world ready for this type of worldwide catastrophe? I would say no . Is anyone preparing to stay here? If you are, be ready to endure an Earth-sized Katrina aftermath.

Do you understand this? Do you have a plan in place for you and your loved ones if they are left here after the Rapture? I am quite aware of the fact that many people don't really believe in the Rapture. I am telling you what I saw and the aftermath. Your life will not be worth much at all. Think about it. All you have to do is accept Jesus Christ as your Lord and Savior and forgive and love each other. These are very simple instructions for you and your loved ones.

Each city or country should have a catastrophe plan available and ready for the people who are left after the Rapture. There should be a centralized place in the city for those who are left to meet. Believe me, from what I saw, your houses will not be safe. The city should have means to contact outside governments with ham radios, shortwave radios, or systems that do not need satellites to work. These governments should be linked to a central location so that everyone will know what is going on around the world. Again, there should be a way to communicate without the use of satellites. Each city should have food and water stored at these locations along with sleeping bags and toiletries. Police officers or military personnel will be needed to staff the safe havens in each city. Prisons should have plans in place to secure prisoners and a means to deter them from escaping. I don't even want to consider how they will be able to do this, especially since there will be an urgency to check on their (the prisoners' and the guards') family members, and the need for self-preservation will be on high alert. Please understand, if you will. Most of you will be left if you do not change. Everyone is in need of a central location to go to be safe and to be able to communicate with the outside world, family, friends, and neighbors.

Does anyone see where this is leading us? One can readily assess the need to have one man who has the means and the authority to organize a world that is teetering on the brink of annihilation—a world that needs to be organized under one system of government to assure that everyone is safe, everyone is fed, and everyone has water to drink. Soon, everyone will pledge an allegiance to this one person.

With this scenario, one can sense that the door will be opened wide for an Antichrist figure that is to be revealed after the Rapture takes place. He will come onto the scene and have all of the answers to unify a world that is in chaos. For each city's own safety, I pray that you organize now and have a police force ready and a form of communication that operates without the need for satellites. Be able to feed your people without them relying on this man of sin who is to come. One must note too that some of the staff of these places may also be raptured. Who do you call on if this happens? Your plans will be out the window. That safe haven may become a trap that evil people may seize and use to make demands. I believe that most of you would prefer the Rapture instead of hell on earth.

During the time that I was left to face the evil here on earth, thoughts of trying to get home and find out if any more of my family were left was an immediate concern. To the people who love and know the Lord, getting home to see who was taken and who was left was of the utmost importance. However, the dangers that existed just outside of the door of my house and within the confines were too grave to comprehend. If people who are left were to find any more of their family, would they be alive? People who did not know the Lord were mean and cruel and were murdering anyone who crossed their path. The enemy was all around me. I could feel evil at every turn. It almost seemed second nature to be mean and evil, to show that one was not weak in order to survive. I could feel the pain and fear of certain death to venture out, but a pressing concern about family made the danger appear less important. But I was wrong. Murder and mayhem were happening all around me. There was total confusion after the Rapture. People were also rampaging through our houses and the streets. I don't know why I was given this revelation, but I do know that there is urgency in this message to let my family and other Christians know what I am experiencing. One often wonders why people are so violent and cruel at a time like this. I would think that this would be a time of mass prayer for forgiveness for those who are left. God once hardened the heart of a pharaoh of Egypt and brought plagues upon the Egyptians. He will also send a delusion upon the people after the Rapture, and they will believe a lie. I can't state this fact enough. Instead of believing the words of people who have seen and heard the word of the Lord, people will believe a lie. Be careful and know where you are going. Again, note 2 Thessalonians 2:10–11. God will send a strong delusion to the unrighteous that received not the truth. For that cause, God will send a strong delusion that they should believe a lie.

Remember—the Lord will send a strong delusion. This is very important. I can't stress enough the way that I felt after witnessing the vision of the Rapture. I awoke in a stupor that day. I was sad and very grieved to know that I could be left here and miss the Rapture because I could not find it in my heart to forgive and love. I started to cry and lament for me, my family, and the human race. I felt a deep and gnawing anger toward myself for not being taken up. It's so simple, Glenda. Just forgive and love. Where are you going?

> *"Knowing this first, that there shall come in the last days scoffers, walking after their own lusts,*
> *"And saying, Where is the promise of his coming? for since the fathers fell asleep, all things continue as they were from the beginning of the creation" (2 Peter 3:3–4).*

Do not be slackers about the coming of the Lord. There will be people poking fun at the fact that the believers are warning of the Rapture. For the day of the Lord will come as a thief in the night for those of you who do not believe. However, He does not come without warnings for His bride, the church. These warnings are all around us. Read the warnings.

Know When the Day of the Lord Is Near

> *"But of the times and the seasons, brethren, ye have no need that I write unto you.*
>
> *"For yourselves know perfectly that the day of the Lord so cometh as a thief in the night.*
>
> *"For when they shall say, Peace and safety; then sudden destruction cometh upon them, as travail upon a woman with child; and they shall not escape.*
>
> *"But ye, brethren, are not in darkness, that that day should overtake you as a thief"* (1 Thessalonians 5:1–4).

The Lord is telling us not to be in darkness about the Day of the Lord. Christians are to know when the day is near. Please read and understand. That day should not overtake Christians as a thief overtakes his victim. Therefore, we should watch and be aware. Know the day is near!

God forgives us time and time again. Therefore, we should also forgive others time and time again. We are not bigger than God. All of your sins can be forgiven with the exception of those who blaspheme against the Holy Ghost, according to Mark 3:29. God doesn't want any of His children to be lost. Now we Christians know that we are to forgive and love one another so that we can be caught up in the air with the Lord instead of being left behind to live a life of sin and fear. That is not a difficult commandment for us to follow: forgive and love. Mark 3:29 states that a person who blasphemes against the Holy Ghost hath never forgiveness, but is in danger of eternal damnation.

I must repeat this. That day should not overtake us as a thief. Read 1 Thessalonians 5:4 again. We are to know when that day is near. It should not overtake us as a thief. We are not in darkness. Are you listening? Know that the day is near! Know that the Day of the Lord is dark. The day of my first vision of the Rapture was not dark, but the second vision was at twilight. I don't know what to make of this as of this moment. Again, I believe the Rapture takes place first, and the Day of the Lord happens afterward.

Many scriptures in the Bible state that the Day of the Lord is a dark day. The sun shall be turned into darkness and the moon into blood. This is why I believe that the Rapture occurs first, and the Day of the Lord occurs afterward. I saw a world that was peaceful and calm before the Rapture during the day and twilight visions, and darkness and terror afterward.

There is deliverance for those left during the Rapture by bowing down and calling on the God of Abraham, Isaac, and Jacob. Whosoever shall call on the name of the Lord shall be delivered, but you will be experiencing the tribulation. At any rate, call on the name of the Lord with love and forgiveness for one another. These are very simple commands to redeem our souls and allow us to be in the Rapture, but what about afterward? Is this the simple rescue plan that all of us want from the horrors of the tribulations to come? Or do you want to continue on the same path and be rescued from increasingly intense disasters? Brothers and sisters in Christ, greed has created a dire worldwide economy that may bring the nations to collapse at any time. Most people don't have the money to prepare for life here after the Rapture. Once the Rapture occurs, total mayhem will rule the world, and people will want your money, food, weapons, and anything else that you have. We need to decide which rescue plan to follow: the Rapture or the horrors left to contend with here on earth. Where are you going?

The Day of the Lord is not a day to rejoice. It is a time of doom and gloom. It is a time of darkness and horror. Please prepare yourselves to be ready for the Rapture or be left here for the Day of the Lord. The Day of the Lord and the Rapture appear to be separate events to me. Sometime after the Rapture occurs, the Day of the Lord will begin. I don't know how long it will be, but it would take another book to talk at length on the subject. In any case, the description above fits so perfectly with the things that I saw. The lands of the world will be lawless if the cities do not take a stand and prepare now because most people will be left here. I know that the Lord is directing us to prepare. All of us must be prepared, in case we do not go up in the Rapture. Every city, county, and state must be prepared for what is about to happen to the world. Again, most people are not ready to go up at this time in their lives, although everyone talks about the Rapture and going up to meet the Lord in the sky. I want to state for you very plainly that if you do not change your ways, you are not going up. At this time, not that many of you will be going up! So, why is there no one planning for the large group of people that will be left here?

The Law and the Prophets Hang on these Commandments

The first and the greatest commandments that were given to the church or Christians by our Lord and Savior Jesus Christ are stated below. How many of us can truly say that we follow these greatest of the commandments in our daily lives? I doubt most Christians are aware of these commandments because they certainly don't adhere to them.

> "Jesus said unto him, Thou shalt love the Lord thy God with all thy heart, and with all thy soul, and with all thy mind.
> "This is the first and great commandment.
> "And the second is like unto it, Thou shalt love thy neighbour as thyself.
> "On these two commandments hang all the law and the prophets" (Matthew 22:37–40).

Jesus left us with the first and greatest commandment, and the second is like unto it. These were similar to the message that I received from the angel. If we abide by these two commandments, we will forgive and love one another. How many people are living by these two commandments? Not the entire Ten Commandments that Moses gave us, but these two simple commandments that Jesus left as our guide to follow. And please note that on these two commandments hang all the law and the prophets. People, this is my message. This was for me. If we live by these two commandments, we will go up in the Rapture.

After noticing these commandments, I was left wondering one day why things were always going wrong for me. My brother reminded me to pray for people who do not like me, people who malign me, and people that I don't care to be around. I thought about this for a moment as he continued to talk. He reminded me that things did not turn around for Job until he prayed for his friends who had believed that their friend, Job, had done something wrong against God to bring on his suffering. Think about this for a moment. Pray for people who misuse you and abuse you. If you have love in your heart for everyone, it is easy to pray for them. This is very important! Please pray for people who harbor bad thoughts against you and attack you verbally or physically.

> *"But I say unto you, Love your enemies, bless them that curse you, do good to them that hate you, and pray for them which despitefully use you, and persecute you" (Matthew 5:44).*

In Matthew 5:44, Jesus is telling us to love our enemies. We are to bless people who curse us. We are to do good to people who hate us. We are to pray for people who despitefully use us and persecute us. I know this may seem extremely difficult for most of you. However, when the Rapture occurs, and you are left here because of holding grudges against people who have hurt you; believe me, those people will not matter. You probably won't see them again because your days will be filled with self-preservation. They will not matter! Forgive them, and pray for them now before it is too late.

Please know that our Father God and Jesus forgive us. Who are we to sit back and judge others? We are not God. We are to do as we are instructed by the words of Jesus and the prophets of the Bible. Love and forgive. If you want the Father to forgive you and take you up in the Rapture, you must abide by His commandments. Loving and forgiving is not that difficult. Do it now.

Please note that it worked for Job, and it can work for you, too. Again, pray for your enemies as well as your family and friends. Do good to those who abuse you. Forgive them and love them. I know that it is hard at first, but that is what you and I must continue to do to be with the Lord. As noted above, you are commanded to love. For all of you hate groups out there, you are in danger of the Lord's wrath. You are commanded to love and not to hate.

Please take the time to learn, heed, and promote the Ten Commandments that the Lord God gave to Moses for the children of Israel. They were mandated then by God, and they are still mandated today for all of us who believe. Many of you have forgotten them and seek to have them dismissed as outdated and not necessary. However, if ever there were a time for the Ten Commandments to be enforced, it is now, at this very time, and wherever you are. These commandments have never gone out of date. The Lord God gave Moses the Ten Commandments. Moses received the Ten Commandments from the Lord and placed them in the Ark of the Covenant for his people to live by, and, to this day, those same commandments are meant for all of God's people to live by, as they did then and should today.

The Lord God of Abraham, Isaac, and Jacob is our God, and there should be no other. Do not bow down to other gods and idols. Do not take the name of the Lord God in vain. Do you hear and understand? Stop using the Lord's name in vain. People seem to do this and get great enjoyment or think that their statements are more persuasive with this vile language added. In addition, the commandment with a promise for long life is to honor thy father and mother. Everyone, notice please, a promise comes with this commandment for longevity. If you honor your father and mother, things may be well with you, and you may live long on the earth. How do some children grow up and think that they are smarter and know more than their parents? Children, you will be wise to stop being disrespectful and dishonest. Listen and beware. And fathers and mothers, you are not to provoke your children to wrath. Bring them up in the nurture and admonition of the Lord. Love them and show them affection. Learn all of the commandments and live by them.

We people on earth make all kinds of pledges. We make pledges to our Gods, our countries, to our flags, and to idols, and the list goes on and on. Even the United States of America has a pledge that is made to our flag. How many people abide by it and follow the rules? Do we honor it the way that it was written: one nation under God, with liberty and justice for all? Does this ring true? What are the first and greatest commandments? Most Christians are not living godly lives. If we are living just and righteous

Christian lives here in America, why did Abraham Lincoln have to set the slaves free? Why couldn't women vote when our country was founded? Why did Lyndon Johnson have to push for a civil rights act? Why did we need affirmative action laws, and on and on …

I can only state things that I know. This is why I have chosen to discuss the confusion that is among Christians living here in America.

The Pledge of Allegiance to the flag reads as follows:

"I pledge allegiance to the flag of the United States of America, and to the republic for which it stands: one nation under God, indivisible, with liberty and justice for all."

What do these words mean? Does any pledge we make mean anything? Think about it. Our words and pledges are all but lost in our lusts of this world. Our word or pledge means nothing to some of us. If we can't remember our pledges, we need to live by God's words in the Bible.

We are to be prepared for the day that we go home to be with the Lord. Will you be a bride who is prepared for the Lamb when He comes? How have you treated your fellow man?

Jesus takes the way that we treat each other here on earth very personally. We were given commandments to treat others as we would ourselves. Jesus actually puts himself in places and conditions that a number of the outstanding law-abiding citizens would find deplorable. Yet, Jesus puts His people on notice: Do you feed the hungry? Have you given water to the thirsty? Have you been kind to a stranger? Have you clothed the naked? Have you visited the sick or visited the prisons? Have you not ministered to any of these? In as much as you do unto these, you do unto Jesus Christ. When one looks down on the people that I mentioned above, who do you think that you are looking down on? Jesus said when you assist these people and minister to them that you are also doing this for Him. I must state that I heard one preacher say that this was only for the Jews, as noted in Matthew 25:35–36. However, I believe it means everyone. I may be wrong, but this is what I feel.

I remember hearing of a church whose members fired their pastor because he allowed the sick and homeless to come into service one Sunday. Here the members sat in their nice clothes and fur coats, and resented the dirty, smelly people coming into their service. People, are you reading your Bible, or the latest fashion trend magazine? And yet, you look for miracles from God. Yet, you believe that you are good Christians. Clothes do not make a Christian! Some people, who are downtrodden, need someone to talk to them to show them the way. One never knows what causes people to become destitute or homeless. A word or a helping hand from a stranger may be the spark that these people need to help them to straighten out their lives. We are to be about our father's business.

Miracles are happening all around us. People often assume that miracles are not real, but if you believe that life is real, then so can miracles be real for you also. As a matter of fact, consider for a moment: Have you ever thought about the dreams that you have at night? Where does your mind go when you are asleep? What do you do when you go to sleep? Where are you, or should I say where are your thoughts being processed? It's interesting to note that God talks to us and shows us dreams and visions during this time. What is it that is so special about the time that we are asleep? This question has always astonished me. There may be answers to this question, but I don't know them at this time. Our minds are in a state that we have no control over during sleep. Maybe this is the reason. This is an attention-grabber for me that the Lord talks to us most often in dreams and visions.

Scientists have come up with all types of names for psychological and mental processes that our brain waves go through. Doctors have given names to the various stages of our mind's rest and sleep processes. There are also names for various illnesses of the mind, such as psychosis, paranoia, and schizophrenia. I don't pretend to know anything about these illnesses, nor do I know anything about people who have been diagnosed. I do know about people who indulge in excessive amounts of alcohol and drugs and some of the problems that they face.

Excessive Drug and Alcohol Use Make Demons Show Up and Show Out

Doctors have been studying our brain functions for years. A number of names have been given to illnesses of the brain. For instance, have you ever seen an alcoholic in delirium tremens (DTs)? As a biologist/chemist and former laboratory technician, I know that DTs is a name that is given to the stage that an alcoholic goes into when he or she is hallucinating or seeing things that we can't see. I have seen several people from my old neighborhood in this stage. I have also seen and talked to a number of drug addicts. For me, the question is how can people who are supposedly having some type of psychosis, in some cases, see the same thing? This has baffled me for years. I have noticed that these people see smiling little people that are trying to harm them. They also see snakes and actually wrestle with these creatures. I remember a person had once run about a mile as he tried to escape the grips of these little people. They came at him with hammers striking hard down around his feet. Another time, a person was wrestling and straining himself as he tried to keep snakes away from his body.

I'd like to make it very clear that I am not a doctor, nor am I an expert in the field of psychology. I am trying to say that there may be another explanation for these visions, and it may be biblical. One may open up the door to Satan and his demons by using drugs and alcohol. Think about it for a moment. Too many people have gotten into trouble and then blamed their actions on drugs and alcohol. Drugs and alcohol in excess open up the door to the dark side. I believe that with all of my heart. I have seen the other side, and it is ugly. Nothing but horror exists there. Satan and his horde are there, and they are busy.

Again, we have all experienced having nightmares and seeing things while we are asleep. Are these things real? Are they an illusion? Where do these images originate? Can a person have a nightmare in the daytime? Does anyone really know where these dreams are coming from? Another question is, Who is playing this motion picture in our heads? People, please note that these images are real to these addicts, and most can relay the events as they saw them.

I have seen alcoholics in various stages of what the doctors refer to as DTs. These, too, are people that I know. Several people have said that they were wrestling with snakes while in DTs. They wrestled with these entities, and they grasped for serpents' heads as they tried to bite them. The head and the tail of the serpent were aggressively trying to wear down the weary prey by biting and whipping the victim's body into an exhaustive state of being. Why a serpent? What is Satan?

On the other hand, a drug addict fights at night with unseen forces and little people who knock him out of bed onto the floor. The addict curses and says the most vulgar and revolting words that can be emitted from a human mouth. He is someone who very seldom curses, someone who walks away from a fight, and who avoids conflicts at all cost. This same person, when confronted, says that he can't remember what is happening, but he stands swinging and fighting unseen forces at night. This same force then begins to come out of that room and begins to knock on a family member's bedroom door. Can evil materialize and be this bold as to come from that room with the drug addict and knock on another door? In addition, the family members would hear two distinct voices during these fights. Let me state this: one family member called the person on his cell phone while he was fighting the demons in his room one night and got a surprise. This person was afraid to go into the room. Therefore, the person made a call to the room, and someone or something answered the telephone, and it was not the family member. Is this one reason to leave drugs and anything that is mind altering alone? I would think so.

Who are these smiling little people that I mentioned earlier? Some people call them imps, haints, genies, demons, wee people, leprechauns, or ghosts. I have also seen these little people, and I was not on any illegal drugs. One was a man who kept grinning at me. I saw him in a vision one night. This little person was trying to intimidate me by following me as I tried to get away from him. Also, I saw one appear in front of me during the night. It appeared as a dark shadow. It slipped through the air and into the bedroom while I was awake. Again, I was awake. This happened in October 2010. The air seemed to ripple or swirl as it did before the angel came through to blow the shofar. It slipped in and tugged at the cover of my bed. I turned to get a better look at it, and it vanished. People, believe me, a number of us are seeing some things that are not of this world. I have heard stories of people grabbing these little people and binding them. As of November 2010, I actually saw an effeminate little person who was trying to get me to engage in a homosexual act. During October 2014, a little girl came to me in a vision, but she would not talk. I studied her, and her eyes began to change, and I immediately knew that she was a demon. Therefore, I asked, "Who are these little people?" I believe they are Satan's minions, and it doesn't matter what names they are called. This is more than a reason to cover you, your family, friends, and enemies with the "blood of Jesus" all day long, and especially at night before you go to bed. Satan comes after people who will expose him. I believe this is why the Bible states that Christians who love the Lord are long-suffering.

Again, some drug addicts realize the same small people beating and striking them as they go into euphoric trances that may be induced by drugs. Why are there snakes and little people? Can they all be the victim of the same psychosis and visualize the same visions? Is this coincidence or imagination playing tricks or, God forbid, demons set loose on a world that has forgotten how easy it is to summon these foul beings? I don't know. But it is time to consider where our minds go when we use any type of mind-altering drugs, such as alcohol, cocaine, crack, heroin, or methamphetamines. This is my thought: I believe that you open up the door to demons, whose only goal is to hurt and to destroy you. We all know that drugs and alcohol do destroy people's lives. Anyway, these demons play with your mind, and you give them an open invitation to your world when you use drugs and alcohol, especially in excess. Have you ever seen a happy drug addict or alcoholic? The Bible states that we suffer from lack of knowledge and the dangers of using drugs). I am going to be bold and add anything that can interfere with one's ability to think clearly.

This leads me to warn the younger generation who are playing by their own rules. The use of drugs and alcohol should not be taken lightly. This generation, I believe, is the show-me generation. They don't believe fire will burn until it burns them. Please know the people who are around you. Don't play follow the leader. You must be your own person and listen to your parents. Be obedient and play by your parents' rules. They know more than you do! You are not smarter or brighter. They kept you safe as babies, and they will help to keep you safe as adults. Listen! I was allowed to see over into the other side, and it is not pretty. I must warn all of you about the things that I saw. Some scary and vile things are on the other side, and you do not want to end up there. Where are you going?

I often asked the question, "Where is the other side?" I have been praying and asking the Lord, "Where are we when we go to the other side?" However, I have not gotten any answers. I really don't know where the other side is or how to get there, with the exception of showing up there while in a vision.

> *"Wine is a mocker, strong drink is raging: and whosoever is deceived thereby is not wise" (Proverbs 20:1).*

> *"Give strong drink unto him that is ready to perish, and wine unto those that be of heavy hearts.*
> *"Let him drink, and forget his poverty, and remember his misery no more" (Proverbs 31:6–7).*

> *"Woe unto them that rise up early in the morning, that they may follow strong drink; that continue until night, till wine inflame them!" (Isaiah 5:11).*

> *"Woe unto them that are mighty to drink wine, and men of strength to mingle strong drink" (Isaiah 5:22).*

Young people are especially fascinated by trying new things. They are experimenting with drugs and alcohol. Please stop it now because you are opening up doors that let demons into this world. Most of you are too young to know about social drinking. You go to the extremes and suffer mightily for your lack of knowledge. I don't believe the verses above need any explanation.

WHY GOD DOESN'T HEAR SOME PRAYERS

God's people are destroyed because we lack knowledge of Him. How many of you have Bibles in your homes? How many times have you walked past them without bothering to pick them up and read them? The word is here. All we have to do is read and ask for understanding from the Lord. We allow things to cloud our minds so that He will not hear us. We also suffer because of our drugs and alcohol excesses: anything that alters the mind to allow Satan and his demons a portal to enter into our minds and hearts. We are destroyed because of our drug use, intoxication, witchcraft, sorcery and magic.

I pray that some of the things that I have mentioned will make a difference in someone's life. It is a good thing to ask for wisdom and understanding when you pray. Ask God to help you pray and understand.

Also, it is a good thing to ask for and have riches on earth, but what about after this earthly life? Look at the pillaging of the tombs of Egypt. Treasures can't be stored up and taken with us. Their treasures were left in the dirt to succumb to time. Note from the past for the present: you can't take it with you! A note to you rich men: What are those riches going to do for you when the Rapture occurs? Why horde your riches and keep them to yourselves? The Lord is watching. He sees and hears.

"And this is the confidence that we have in him, that, if we ask any thing according to his will, he heareth us:

> *"And if we know that he hear us, whatsoever we ask,*
> *we know that we have the petitions that we desired of him"*
> *(1 John 5:14–15).*

According to 1 John 5:14–15, we should have confidence in the fact that if we ask anything of the Lord according to his will, He will hear us. If we believe that He hears us, we should have what we desire of him. Isaiah 59:2 states that our iniquities separate us from God and our sins make Him hide His face so that He cannot hear us. If there is hate in your heart, the Lord God will not hear you. The Lord does not hear us if we ask amiss. We cannot ask for the Lord to supply us with lustful pursuits of the heart. Note below.

> *"Ye ask, and receive not, because ye ask amiss, that ye may consume it upon your lusts" (James 4:3).*

> *"My people are destroyed for lack of knowledge: because thou hast rejected knowledge, I will also reject thee, that thou shalt be no priest to me: seeing thou hast forgotten the law of thy God, I will also forget thy children" (Hosea 4:6).*

Again, "My people are destroyed for lack of knowledge: because thou hast rejected knowledge," according to Hosea. We are destroyed, not hurt or punished, but, destroyed for lack of knowledge. We suffer for our use of drugs, alcohol, witchcraft, sorceries, idol worship, hatred, and unforgivingness and for not being good stewards of the many blessings that we have. People, think for yourselves for one moment. You can't create magic and conjure up spirits. You are not that powerful, but Satan is. He can give you this power if you tap into his dark world. There is no difference in calling witchcraft black and white. Both are evil and are of Satan. Please, leave it alone. Read the Bible and get the knowledge of God in your heart.

Did you know that the Lord can hate? There are lists below. Note also that there are works of the flesh that are not pleasing to Him. If you are doing the things on these lists, you are separating yourself from God. Know for sure that God will not hear you. Take note of Proverbs and Galatians below.

> *"These six things doth the LORD hate: yea, seven are an abomination unto him:*

> "*A proud look, a lying tongue, and hands that shed innocent blood,*
> "*An heart that deviseth wicked imaginations, feet that be swift in running to mischief,*
> "*A false witness that speaketh lies, and he that soweth discord among brethren*" (Proverbs 6:16–19).

> "*Now the works of the flesh are manifest, which are these; Adultery, fornication, uncleanness, lasciviousness,*
> "*Idolatry, witchcraft, hatred, variance, emulations, wrath, strife, seditions, heresies,*
> "*Envyings, murders, drunkenness, revellings, and such like: of the which I tell you before, as I have also told you in time past, that they which do such things shall not inherit the kingdom of God*" (Galatians 5:19–21).

Instead of using drugs and alcohol, get your mind and body right to take communion. My family started to take communion every day after the visions started coming. Jesus gave us the reason we are to take communion until he comes. The Bible explains the Bible. It can't be made any clearer than this. Let me state very clearly here that some of us are sick for many reasons, but the Bible gives us one explanation here.

Many of us are weak and sickly because we have not discerned the Lord's body. We don't acknowledge that the Lord died on the cross for our sins. We don't break His Bread and drink His Blood on a daily basis. I have also heard preachers and evangelist noting the same thing on television. It makes me want to ask the question, "Are we seeing the same things? And is the Lord speaking and showing us the same things?" I take communion daily, when I know that my heart is right. Let's face it, people. Sometimes the heart is weak and not right with God.

There are also people who are sick because they brought it on themselves, maybe by using drugs or through some form of sexual acts. It is good to know that we have a Savior, Who has already paid the price for our sins. He died on the cross to save us from our sins, and we take communion by symbolically drinking His blood and eating His body to heal our bodies from all illnesses and diseases, regardless of who we are.

Jesus stated that we should take communion in remembrance of Him. As often as we take it, we show His death until He comes back. We are to examine ourselves before we take it. If we are unworthy, we are guilty of the body and blood of the Lord Jesus Christ. Many people are weak and sick. Be careful when you take communion. Your hearts must be right with God.

Sometimes we get upset with the Lord because sickness and bad things happen to us. Again, the Lord will chastise those whom He loves. Have you ever just wondered why you have to suffer so much? You look around and see that the people who are doing evil continue to do evil, and it appears that nothing ever really happens to them. Again, the Lord can take his hedge from around you, just as he did with Job. When the hedge is gone, the devil can have his way. All of you who love the Lord have felt at one time or another like the Lord has given you over to Satan. No matter how much we think that this world is about us, we continue to come back to the fact that it is about God and our Lord and Savior Jesus Christ.

Shall we receive good at the hand of God, and shall we not receive evil is a question that Job asked his wife. In all that happened to Job, he did not speak harshly or sin with the words from his mouth. It is all too often that we feel that good should happen to us at all times. But if you are truly a Christian, there will always be good times mixed with the bad. The disciples and the early church suffered tremendous burdens. These are the same men and women who were with Christ and saw all of the wonderful miracles that our Lord and Savior performed. They had firsthand knowledge of Jesus Christ and knew that He was the Son of the most High God. Are people who have had more tribulations and problems better Christians than those who have not been chastened by the Lord? Are those who have more problems in this world more blessed? I don't know the answer but want to give you a cause to think for a moment. The Lord stated that He came to bring division, not peace on earth, the first time that He came. I think that the division was to try His saints in the fire as he tried Abraham with Isaac (some of you may want to read the story). Peace will be with Jesus when He comes back the second time to reign.

PEEPING AND COMMUNICATING BEYOND THE VEIL

My mother passed in March of 2004. This was very hard for me, and I really thought that I would stop breathing if she passed. However, about three months after she passed, I saw her in a vision. She came back to a house that we were cleaning. This house had live birds in the windows. At any rate, I feel the house was a reference to our spiritual house, which is our soul. It was symbolic of a spiritual body that needed to be cleaned. That was the message that I got about the house at that time. Nevertheless, I looked at my mother and said, "Mama, how can you be here? You died." She said, "They told me that I could come back." I said, "But, you've been dead for about three months. I could understand it better if you had died last night and the doctors made a mistake and you were really alive." Again, she said, "They told me that I could come back." I was motionless and perplexed. My mother was alive and walking around in this vision. I spoke again and said, "Jesus Christ is the only person that I know was resurrected. How can you be here?" Again, she said, "They told me I could come back." Let me add that there are, however, others in the Bible who were raised from the dead. At any rate, I said to my mother, "I'm tired, and I've got to sit down to think this over." At that point, when I sat down in the vision, I woke up and knew immediately that this vision was a right-here and right-now moment.

On January 16, 2012, my mother came back to me in a vision. She was in a huge house that needed cleaning again. The house was extremely large, and we needed escalators to move around in it. This house also had birds down on the floor around my mother's feet. I stooped down to shoo the birds away and found a huge bat among them. It was frightening to see this huge bat with the birds. My mother stood perfectly motionless and silent while I was in a state of panic. I repeatedly told my mother that we needed to get the birds and bat out of the house. However, my mother was immovable. I woke up from this vision trying to figure out the meaning because my mother never spoke. Since my first vision of my mother was that of a dirty house with birds and a message to clean our souls, I believe that my mother was saying that our houses or souls needed more work because the enemy (Satan) is raging. We need to concentrate on keeping our spiritual houses clean.

For anyone to understand this, first, one would have to know my mother. She loved her children more than she loved herself. I remember one of her friends stating, "I can't understand how a person can spoil all of her children, but you have done it." My mother would have found a way to come back to us and talk to us if there was a way possible, and it appears to me that that is exactly what happened. Maybe.

On another note, an ex-boyfriend of mine died a year or so after my mother. Three weeks after he had died, I had a vision of him one night as I slept alone in my bed. My husband was out of town. This person's face came through the darkness of my bedroom in the vision. I will not state what was said or what transpired, but we had a short conversation, which could only have been stated at that time, after his death. I value my privacy in this matter. Some things are not meant to be repeated. Anyway, his face went back into the darkness after we talked, and the veil was opened for just a moment, and I could see him sitting in a chair. Millions of people were sitting around in chairs with him. I got the message that he was in a type of waiting area, but the veil closed, and he could not hear me as I spoke to him again. I have heard other people on Christian television talk about this topic of a waiting area outside of the gates of heaven where the first judgment takes place. I don't know where he was, but he was definitely outside in a waiting area. One minute he was in my room, and the next he was sitting in a waiting area and appeared to have been there for some time. Let me state here too, that he was much younger. At any rate, I think it is safe to say that time is not relevant once a person leaves this world. This is why a day can be like a thousand years with the Lord, and a thousand years like one day.

It wasn't long after this vision that my mother came back again in another vision. I told her that my ex-boyfriend had died and came to me in a vision. My mother said, "When did he die?" I said, "About three weeks ago (this was true)." My mother said, "What did he say?" I told her what he said. My mother and I had this conversation about this person like we were talking when she was alive. Amazing.

I saw visions of my ex-boyfriend about the summer of 2007 (I think). He was with my mother and stepfather (my dad), who had passed in 1986. My dad was a person who was full of laughter and who loved to have fun. In the vision, my dad was staring at me with a grin on his face, while my mother and ex-boyfriend were looking at something on a table behind him. My mother's back was to me and my ex-boyfriend was standing with a profile of his face showing as he watched my mother doing something at a table. My dad appeared to be the only person who was aware that I was watching them, for he was looking directly at me with a wide grin on his face. My dad always had this same grin on his face at Christmas when he wanted to tell whose name he had chosen to buy a gift but could not. He appeared to be overly enthusiastic to tell a secret that he should not. On the other hand, the room was muted in brightness. I do believe with all of my heart that this was a Gold Room in heaven where I saw my mother, stepfather, and ex-boyfriend. I have heard about these rooms with tables and books on them. The deceased can use these books to send messages back to the living here on earth. This is something that I have heard, and it is similar to what I saw. Again, I can only tell you what I saw. This may not be true about a Gold Room in heaven. I just don't know at his time.

During September 2011, I had a vision of a relative who had died about eight years ago. This person was sitting in a straight chair, and a lot of artificial light was shining on him. Also, a number of people were behind him, but I could not distinguish their faces. At any rate, I went to see this person a couple of months before he died in 2003, and he accused me of something that I had no clue about at the time. This worried me because I did not know why he would state something about me that was not true. However, I did not question anyone at that time, but later I told several relatives about what had transpired. Also, I became quite disturbed about his statement while talking to someone before I had this vision. However, in the vision, this person came back to me and told me exactly what had happened and why he said what he did. Now, mind you, he came back to me just to let me know why he had stated this. The statement that he had made came from a lie that another relative had stated to him. Therefore, I confronted the relative and told the person exactly what had been stated in the vision. This person could not deny anything that I had revealed, and the person has not apologized at the time of this publication. Amazing? I think so. I continue to ask why this person had to come back and explain to me why he was acting mean before he died. At any rate, there have been others to come back after they have died to set things right with me too. I really don't know why; nor do I know what all of this means at this time.

A Message for Abortionists

Let me add something else that I saw. The vision that I saw of a waiting area for people who had died gave me another surprise. I saw a baby in this waiting area. For all of the people who advocate abortion rights, I ask a question of you. Where do you think your children have gone once they cease to exist? Do they go back to the dirt? Do you hide them in the doctor's office? Does the doctor hide them for you? Where are they? Look at the number of abortions that are happening.

Here is a little note: Herod set a decree in the Holy Land to kill babies around the time that Jesus was born. One might say that this was Jesus's First Coming. Today, we have a law to kill babies again. Women have the right to have abortions. One might say that we are preparing for Jesus Christ's Second Coming. Does anyone see the irony here? There are parents killing children, and children killing parents. The Bible stated that these things would happen over two thousand years ago. A world full of confusion is here, and Satan is the author of confusion.

All of you people who are pro-choice, please reconsider your views. Aborted babies are also in a place that God has reserved for them. I saw what I thought was an aborted baby, one that was "unborn." This is the actual term that came into my head: the word *unborn*. I asked a question about this child, and the words came from someone beyond the veil that it was "unborn." As a Christian, think about this for a moment. A body, soul, and spirit inhabit the bodies of all of us on the earth. To abort a baby here on earth at any stage of development is to get rid of the body, soul, and spirit of that child. The body can be destroyed, but the soul and the spirit must go back to the place from which they came, and I do believe strongly that that place is in heaven. Is it convenient to get rid of an unwanted baby? I don't have all of the answers, but those babies' spirits and souls have to go back to heaven from whence they came, just as our spirits must go somewhere when we, adults, die. They don't just disappear. My God … my God … stop what you are doing to these babies. I think you will see them again. The one I saw in the waiting area was a girl (this is what I believe) with a shade of hair that I have never seen on earth. Again, the message was, "She is unborn." Something did not look right with this child. She looked as though she was mentally challenged. I, in turn, started to assume and make notes in this book that this child was aborted. However, as I question the message and try to be precise with all details, I can't say that this is a fact. I can state for the record that this is what I felt in my heart. In addition, I might add that this is a strong feeling today as I continue to write. This is why I am leaving the notes about this "unborn" child as I have written them above because the Lord hates shedding of innocent blood.

When an egg is fertilized, it contains a soul and a spirit that will become a person (body, soul, and spirit). It is alive and begins a transformation cycle to become human. The soul and the spirit can't be killed, but the body can. If you don't remember anything else, please remember the soul and spirit can't be killed on this earth. So I pose this question to you again: Where does that child go? Let me just share this with you again. I saw what I thought was an aborted baby in this waiting area. I even got the message "unborn" in my head. Was this child aborted or not allowed to live? Why was this child in this waiting area, and why did she look as though she was not physically or mentally whole? It doesn't matter, because I know a truth that I strongly believe. Aborted children will face all of you mothers again when we stand to be judged. Aborted children are waiting for you.

Another interesting note about this child is the color of her hair. This child's hair was a red color that one doesn't see here on earth. This redheaded child was unborn, according to someone beyond the veil. I called this child a girl because she had so much hair. It may have, indeed, been a boy. I only felt that the child was a girl. Why was this unborn child here? Is it waiting to be reborn at some time in the future? Within the past year, I have heard on Christian television that redheaded people are getting ready to be reborn to populate the earth again. Who is this child, and what does unborn mean? I don't know at this time. You may want to research for yourself. I pray that I am not inserting too much of my beliefs into this book as I try to reveal facts to my reader. I ask the Lord God of Abraham, Isaac, and Jacob to forgive me if I am.

> *"Dearly beloved, avenge not yourselves, but rather give place unto wrath: for it is written, Vengeance is mine; I will repay, saith the Lord" (Romans 12:19).*

This is also a clear message to all of the people who want to seek revenge on abortion practitioners, or on anyone. Please know that these children are already with the Lord (according to my belief). Revenge "is" the Lord's. We are to love and forgive on this earth. As true Christians, we can't lie in wait to take a life to make amends for something that has been done here on earth. The Lord sees, and He knows. There are watchers and Holy Ones. Someone is making notes about you too at all times. It is time for Christians to behave like Christians. Know your God. He is a God of love. People are behaving like "lynch mobs" when they go after people who are committing these acts. This is not the true nature of a Christian. Remember that we are not to "judge" others. We are not gods and do not have any power over people. Christians do not stand out in front of people's homes to condemn them for something that the court is deciding. Let the courts do their jobs. The courts have a judge and a jury to make decisions. What has gone wrong with the world? People, are you listening?

> *"Judge not, that ye be not judged.*
> *"For with what judgment ye judge, ye shall be judged: and with what measure ye mete, it shall be measured to you again" (Matthew 7:1–2).*

Additionally, God is telling all of us to repent. If you young and old people repent of your fornications, this will stop a number of unwanted pregnancies from occurring. There is no reason to be ignorant of the fact that some, not all, abortions can be prevented just by obeying the Lord and repenting of fornications. Fornication is described as having sex without being married. Where are you going?

Surviving the Time of Testing Like Job

I have been through a lot, and I have seen several visions during the past years. I guess that I can go back to childhood to let you know that these visions are not something that is new to me. I always felt that I could hear something breathing in a bedroom of a relative's house when I was approximately three or four years old. There were times that I would go into the room, and I could feel the presence of something in there with me. One night, my mother put me and my older brother to bed in that room. We had to be three and four years old respectively. My mother closed the door slightly and left the room. Suddenly, this boisterous, overpowering, extremely piercing, and evil laughter shook the foundations of the house. My brother and I were frightened to no end. We cowered under the covers knowing that at any second our mother would come and rescue us. We clung to each other not knowing what to do. Finally, I said to my brother, "Let me get on the back side of the bed so that the devil won't get me." He said something to the effect that he was as afraid as I was. We wondered where our mama was, and what was taking her so long to come to our rescue. But mama never came. She didn't even hear it, and she was sitting in the next room near the door. If ever there was a thought in my head that Satan was real, I knew at that very moment that something evil had confronted us.

No one else heard the evil laughter that shook the entire room that we were in that night. How was that possible? Even today, I shudder when I bring to remembrance the evil that we heard that night.

Since this is my story, and I am trying to lay down some background about the visions that my family and I have seen, I will not include too much information about others. I do, however, want to share a night of horror with you that my daughter and I experienced when my daughter was about eleven years old. I had put her to bed for the night. After about two hours, she came to my bedroom in tears. She said, "I had a dream that a demon just came to me in a red dress. He was a man, but he was wearing a red dress. He said in a whisper, 'I'm coming to get you.'" He also followed her around wherever she went in this dream. My daughter said that she picked up some anointing oil and started sprinkling it on the demon while she was crying out, "The blood of Jesus! The blood of Jesus! The blood of Jesus!" She stated that the demon then disappeared but left his dress behind on the floor.

Now this story that she told me was certainly scary, to say the least. I calmed my daughter down. Then I began to wonder how she knew about anointing oil. Yes, we went to church every Sunday and were faithful members. Going to church and knowing about the power of anointing oil is something else. I could not readily remember if this was something that the pastor talked about at length, nor could I ever remember my daughter being anointed with oil or being taught this. Some churches have gotten away from covering themselves in the blood and providing the congregation with the knowledge of the anointing. We need to get back to the Bible and to putting on the full armor of God. I anoint with oil before I pray most days.

Anyway, I calmed my daughter down and told her to sleep with me. I left the light and the television on in the bedroom. Alone and frightened, we started to drift off to sleep after some time. Suddenly, my daughter sat up in the bed and began to cry again. She was quite inconsolable at this point. She said that the demon came back. He was wearing a blue lace dress this time. He told her, "Your mama can't help you. Don't call your mama this time. I'm coming to get you." The only time that I remember Satan being assured that he had control of a person's life is with Job. The backdrop to this story is that my daughter loved the Lord as a child. She loved to go to church, and started singing the songs before she could talk. Her entire life was centered on the Lord. When she started school, she would preach to her classmates, and her teacher would call me and tell me to make her stop. Now, my daughter's life has certainly been like Job's, and the Lord seems to have a special protection over her. Therefore, people, beware. Some people who have harmed her have met the wrath of God too.

Nevertheless, going back to that night, these visions were too much for us to deal with in one night. We both needed answers as to what was happening. Therefore, I went to church with a girlfriend of mine. Her pastor took one look at me and told me a number of things about me that were true. He told me what was in my pocket. He also told me that there was something over my house that needed to be removed. I don't know if witchcraft was at work during this time. However, I must admit that I was terrified by this ordeal.

Let me summarize this for a moment. My daughter saw a demon that was a man and purposefully wearing dresses. She was young and quite confused about this demon, which looked like a man but was wearing a dress. And at the time, I had no clue as to the meaning. The answer came to me almost thirty years later. I was sitting on a beach in the Caribbean. The Lord spoke to me and said, "Remember the demon who was wearing the dress that came to your daughter? There are men and women wearing each other's clothing today. There are people of the same sexual orientation sleeping with each other. It is demonic." I was startled and could not move after the Lord spoke. It had taken all of these years for me to get an answer about this demon, and it came to me at that moment. People, do you understand? The Lord said that it is demonic. Note Leviticus.

> *"Thou shalt not lie with mankind, as with womankind: it is abomination.*
>
> *"Neither shalt thou lie with any beast to defile thyself therewith: neither shall any woman stand before a beast to lie down thereto: it is confusion"* (Leviticus 18:22–23).

> *"If a man also lie with mankind, as he lieth with a woman, both of them have committed an abomination: they shall surely be put to death; their blood shall be upon them"* (Leviticus 20:13).

> *"And if a man lie with a beast, he shall surely be put to death: and ye shall slay the beast"* (Leviticus 20:15).

> *"Know ye not that the unrighteous shall not inherit the kingdom of God? Be not deceived: neither fornicators, nor idolaters, nor adulterers, nor effeminate, nor abusers of themselves with mankind" (1 Corinthians 6:9).*

This message was placed on my heart while I was vacationing during the fall of 2010. The vision came back to me as though it had just happened. People, I was on vacation while sitting on the beach when this vision came to me. It took almost thirty years for the answer to come to me about this demon, but the answer did come. My eyes were opened, and the Lord told me that this demon was a sexual demon that was encouraging people to commit homosexual acts. The Lord told me to go back to this manuscript and state how this demon appeared to my daughter and to write what He had told me. Again, I can only state what we have seen, heard, and experienced. Please note that this message was a strong charge for me to cite here. I believe this country has passed a law giving Satan and his demons a stronghold in our land. The courts have committed an abomination toward the God of Abraham, Isaac, and Jacob. However, we are not to condemn anyone. We are to love, forgive, and promote Christian values.

Many jealous people have wanted evil to happen to me and my family over the years. Jealousy can kill the souls of people. There were people around me in my past who wanted me to fail in everything that I tried. Some of these people have died and have come back to me in dreams and visions to be reacquainted or to apologize. This is a fact. People who could bring such a damnable and hellish nightmare into the lives of me and my children are only capable of living their miserable lives through hatred and fear. They have a damnable cross to bear. Although I continue to have thoughts about these people, I had to let it go and start to forgive and to love.

I did not know that people could actually work evil on people who did not believe in this sort of thing. I was naïve to think that one had to believe in this evil for it to work. And, at the time, I did not believe in it. However, not only can people do evil things to you, but they can do it to children, too. Here is an added note. My son was with a babysitter who gave an item of his to another person. Soon after the item was given away, my son began to see snakes in the bed at night. We could not think straight, nor did we have much peace of mind during this time. But we held on to God for strength. The love of the Lord kept us strong and encouraged. I just could not fathom the number of evil people who wanted harm to come to me. People of God, remember that the Lord will fight these battles for us. Evil does not triumph forever.

People, you need to be aware of the power of evil. It can cause you all sorts of pain. Open up your hearts and let the Holy Spirit come to live in you. Keep your home safe and secure. I cover me, my family, my friends, enemies, and our homes and possessions with the blood of Jesus all day long.

Let me acquaint you with another night of horror that my daughter and I experienced. My daughter ran into my bedroom one night and said that something was in her room, and it tried to choke her. I was really sleepy that night, but I am a strong person in the ways of the Lord now. I told my daughter to sleep with me, and I would deal with it the next day. I usually anoint my windows and doors and pray for safety, but I wanted to confront the evil that had scared my child. Therefore, I told her to sleep in my bed that night, and I wanted to sleep in hers the next night. Believe me, people, with all that I have seen, I am not as afraid of Satan and his demons as I was in the past. At any rate, I woke up late in the night and heard deep breathing on the pillow next to me. It was very loud and almost sounded like someone snoring. I said, "I hear you. I'm not afraid of you. You must leave my house in the name of Jesus because I am sleepy, and I am going to sleep." And, that is exactly what I did. I turned over and went to sleep. The next day, I prayed over my house and anointed it with oil. Remember—Satan has to flee when we use the name of Jesus. And fear is of Satan, not the Lord. That was the first and last time that my daughter had that experience.

CITY OF DEMONS

This next vision frightened me so that I have tried for several years now to get it out of my head. This happened before I became as strong in the Lord as I was in the previous paragraph. However, since I have tried to convey to you the magnitude and depth of evil and the lengths that people will go to bring harm to someone, I believe that it is now time for me to acquaint you with an evil that I pray to God that I will never encounter again. People are vicious, and some of them will go to new lengths to do you harm. This is why we all must pray and cover ourselves with the blood of Jesus every day. I believe that the Lord allowed me to actually see how evil works in the spirit world in this vision. The Lord allowed me to see the people who were causing me harm, encounter this evil, become acquainted with it, and know that it was wrought by Satan. This evil was scarier than any horror movie.

It was on a Saturday in the summer of 2005. I received a vision in which I was taken to a place by someone I knew. Again, I put forth a question. Where does one actually go in a vision? This place looked like a city or town that one would see in America. However, I can testify that I was not anywhere near home or in a place that was familiar. Anyway, this person took me to a set of rowhouses that was somewhere outside of "my" city. The ground was very craggy and uneven. We walked for some time, trying desperately to steady ourselves on this unholy ground. How I knew it was unholy is a mystery to me. I just knew. We ended up at a home of a male friend of this acquaintance. This male friend had a number of males in the house, and, now, I can't remember what they were doing. I think they had been playing cards. My acquaintance went up to the man of the house, and they whispered something to each other. I waited at the door of the house for them to come to me. My acquaintance came back to me with a whole ham wrapped in aluminum foil. Sliced tomatoes and lettuce were thrown haphazardly around the ham. My acquaintance handed the foil to me and left. The backdrop to this story is that just days before, I had had a ham sandwich in the presence of someone whose family is noted for trying to work evil on people. Anyway, I left this man's house, and I found myself walking alone around this rugged terrain for what seemed to be hours trying to find my acquaintance so that I could go home. At some point, I realized that I no longer had the foil with the ham. I walked until I found this overly friendly girl who was too willing to get me to go to her room so that I could use her telephone to call someone to come to this place and take me home. I will call the girl Smiley because that is what she did the entire time. Anyway, I took her up on the offer. The girl's room was small and dark except for a lamp that sat on a table on the left side of the room. The other side of the room was very dark and foreboding. A woman sat there on the other side of the room with her back to me. I asked, "Who is that woman?" Smiley said, "Oh that's my roommate." I don't remember all of the conversation, but Smiley stated that her roommate did not mind me being there. Smiley kept grinning as she kept stating that she would get me home. I told her that I wanted to go to _____, which is where I live in North Carolina. I said to Smiley, "I see you don't have a telephone, so how are you going to help me get a ride back to _____?" I told her that I was too tired to walk anymore, but I knew I had to get out of her room. It was so frightening to stand there and see her roommate shrouded in darkness. The roommate never turned to look at me face to face. After a while, I left the room with Smiley in tow. All the while, Smiley was saying, "I'm going to get you home." I told Smiley, "Just call me a cab; I don't care how much it will cost me, because I will pay anything to get back to _____, North Carolina." Smiley and I walked down to a corner, and a car drove up to the curb. I can't say what kind of car it was, for legal reasons, and at that time, I had never seen a car like that. I did not pay much attention to it at the time, but later I noticed that Smiley and I were standing at a curb that was near a crossroads. In folklore, the crossroads is the place to meet Satan at midnight if you want power from him. Anyway, Smiley pointed to the car, which had four, yes, four, demons in it. They almost looked like zombies because their eyes had dark rings around them. They were more like painted continuous circles. Their skin was a grayish dull color, and they did not have on clothes, because they looked alien-like. They were about three feet tall. They actually looked like alien beings that I have seen portrayed in movies. I first stated that they looked like zombies because of their eyes. However, they really looked like the aliens that are in the movies and on television. The only difference was that they had small round heads in proportion to their bodies. I feel safe in saying that these may be the demons that people are calling aliens. I truly believe that aliens and demons are the same after seeing these beings. Nonetheless, Smiley said to me, "Get in the car with them; they will take you home." I was terrified at the sight before me. I said, "No; I need to find a telephone and call a cab to get home to _____." The demons, for some reason, would not look at me. I get chills as I describe them now. They looked straight ahead and would not turn their heads to look at me or Smiley. "Go ahead and get into the car with them; they will take you home," said Smiley. "No!" I declared. "I need to get to a telephone to call me a cab." I was afraid that darkness would come soon because the sun had started to set. And I did not want darkness to find me in this place.

I awoke from this out-of-body experience drained and exhausted. I had walked with these demons and experienced this in another time and dimension, and when I returned to my room, I found myself washed out from the ordeal. I could not get out of the bed that day. My very energy had been depleted and used up. I could barely get up to go to the restroom. It was late that night before I could muster up enough energy to get out of bed and eat.

Let me add something here. I am writing this on November 12, 2010. In the vision mentioned above, two families were involved in this evil against me on this day. I actually saw one person (the one who took me there), and I knew of the other family's involvement. Again, there is only good and evil in this world. The Lord allowed me to experience this evil in real time, and it made me a believer of evil that people are capable of conjuring.

People, beware with whom you keep company. Additionally, the car that I saw was real. I am not that much into cars and never paid that much attention to them. However, it is a car that is sold by an American company, and it is a car that one doesn't see very often. The backstory to the car is, when I actually saw a car like that on the street one day, I almost wrecked. I started to scream and say that the car was real. It is a very unique car, and I have only seen one like it in my small city, but since then, I have seen similar cars on television. Believe me, there are people out there who can conjure up demons and send you to places that you don't want to go. I received the message that a fight is going on between the forces of good and evil for our souls and that there are people who can tap into those forces to cause harm to come to you. The Lord allowed me to look into this realm and experience firsthand the battle that is taking place in the spirit realm. The Bible states emphatically that we are not to deal with familiar spirits. After reading this experience that I had, I think you can see why the Lord forbids this. The following are verses in the Bible that forbid anyone from dealing with these spirits.

> "*Regard not them that have familiar spirits, neither seek after wizards, to be defiled by them: I am the LORD your God*" *(Leviticus 19:31).*

> "*And the soul that turneth after such as have familiar spirits, and after wizards, to go a whoring after them, I will even set my face against that soul, and will cut him off from among his people*" *(Leviticus 20:6).*

> "*And when they shall say unto you, Seek unto them that have familiar spirits, and unto wizards that peep, and that mutter: should not a people seek unto their God? for the living to the dead?*" *(Isaiah 8:19).*

People, I can only state that this was real and that someone tapped into that realm and sent me to a very real and evil city of demons. Notice how Isaiah states that wizards can peep and mutter. However, as evil as this place was, I thank God for not letting me get into that car with those demons. I was very aware of everything that was happening in this vision too. I think God allowed me to see this, to witness the differences in the demons, and to let me know how demons work on the other side. For people who are involved in this, it is not too late to stop this madness if you are involved with this sort of thing; give it up and give God the glory. He is the God of truth and miracles. Yes, Satan can work miracles, but the Bible states that he will not stand.

THE HOLY SPIRIT SPEAKS THROUGH ME

I wasn't going to put this in the book, but I think that I should because the power of the Holy Spirit should be known. I will try to keep the story short because I dream movie-length visions. I'll try to give the short version. My daughter had a friend of which not too many of my family was fond, but didn't know why. I told my daughter that there was something about this girl that I just could not put my finger on at that time and truthfully say that this is what I don't like about her. My daughter saw her as a good friend and liked being around her, but there was just something there that I did not like. I prayed and asked the Lord to reveal to me what it was about this person that I didn't care for. Later, I had a vision of being in something like a hotel with celebrities, and we were all sitting around talking. My son came into the room, and I left to go get my daughter. The building was a maze of rooms, just like a hotel. After awhile, I ended up in the back of the building on the second floor. There was a loading dock on this floor with a metal door that slid up and down like those in a warehouse leading outside. I stood there looking at the door and noticed several pieces of dried-up matter scattered across the floor leading to the door. In the room on the left sat a man whose nationality was not American. He was reading something and spoke with an accent. I asked him, "Have you seen my daughter come down this way?" He said, "Yes, she's getting into the car with some people who are outside." I could see the door but did not want to walk on the dried matter on the floor. I asked the man, "What are these things on the floor?" He said, "They are snakes. They come in here all the time." At that point, I felt terror. I am deathly afraid of snakes. I knew that I had to get to my daughter, but I didn't want to walk over the snakes. I looked down at my feet and realized that my feet were suddenly bare. Well, I put my fear aside and ran across the floor to the door to see several people walking my daughter to a white _____ car. Anyway, I noticed that I was on the second floor looking out over the roof of the first floor. My daughter and these people were in a parking lot directly below me. I tried to call out to my daughter, but every time I tried to call her name, a loud horn would blow. I don't know how many times I tried to call out to her, but each time the horn would blow and drown out my voice. This is why it is important to write down visions and dreams immediately. Since my daughter could not hear me, she was led to the car (again, a car is involved). Evidently, demons must have a need for some mode of transportation, or UFOs. Anyway, she got into the back of the car with the people. I stood there in horror as the car drove off with her in it. I awoke from this vision exhausted. I tried to sit up in bed and call my daughter, who was in another room getting ready for work. I kept calling her name until I mustered up enough strength for her to hear me. I wanted to tell her that she was being led to hell. That is the message that was on my heart, although no one told me this. I felt that she was on her way to hell. After some time, my daughter came to my bedroom door and asked if I called her. The words poured out of my mouth, and this is what I said: "You're going to move in with her … you're going to move in with her!" My daughter looked at me astonished and said, "It's a possibility." I said, "I am not saying that, because that is not what I saw." I then said, "I don't know where those words are coming from. That is not me talking." I frantically repeated the words above several times.

Nonetheless, my daughter said that she and this girl had thought about moving in together. I told her my vision and fears about her being led to hell. I tried to tell her that that was not me talking when the words "you're moving in with her" came out of my mouth. At any rate, my daughter could not understand what was so wrong with this person, but I told her that she needed to really reconsider her thoughts of moving in with this person because I believe that the Holy Spirit spoke to her. He used my voice to speak those words because that is not what I was going to say. I think the Holy Spirit gave me a vision; He interpreted it, and He delivered the interpretation by using my voice. Believe me, that is not what I saw! At any rate, my daughter could not believe that her friend was being taken away from her without an explanation. However, she decided not to move in with this person while remaining close friends. I, however, remained in awe of having these words come out of my mouth. When I saw that the friendship was continuing, I prayed and asked the Lord to intercede and tell my daughter that she could not be friends with this girl, and I asked Him to speak to my son also to bring the family as close as we could be in these last days. The Lord wasted no time in talking to my daughter. He spoke to her in a vision within days. My daughter had fallen asleep in the basement on a couch in the den. She has never done this before. However, the Lord came to her during the night while she was in the den. He told her, "Your mother asked me to come to you and tell you that you can't be friends with this girl anymore. I want you to go to your mother and tell her that I did what she asked of me." My daughter stated that after all of this, she did not want to tell me about the Lord's visitation. The Lord sensed her frustration and took her, literally, by the collar of her shirt in the vision and put her in front of me in my dining room within a second, or the twinkling of an eye. He then said to her, "Tell your mother that I did exactly what she asked of me, and I told you why you could not be friends with this girl." My daughter then told me, while in the vision, that she knew why she could not be friends with this girl and that the Lord told her to tell me this fact. I, in turn, told her, "I know … I know." Now, when she awoke from this vision, my daughter told me that she continued to be hesitant about telling me that the Lord visited her and told her to tell me that He had done what I had asked, and now she knew why she could not be friends with this girl. However, she did as she had done in the vision and told me that the Lord had done what I asked. Amazing what the Lord will do for you if you ask, isn't it?

On the other hand, the Lord sent the voice of my deceased mother to speak to my son. My mother's voice told my son that he needed to bring the family together and that we would not prosper until this happens. Praise God!

On February 23, 2009, at approximately 7:00 p.m., I heard my deceased mother's voice call out to me and say, "Glenda." I was awake and sitting in a chair in my bedroom while reading the newspaper when this happened. I heard her voice loud and clear. This actually kept me awake all night because I don't know why I heard her voice call to me. I continue to ask for understanding from God. Was this a warning of some sort? I did not answer her, because I know we are not to speak or communicate with the dead. I can't control visions, but I can control my actions while I am awake. Recently, I heard a prophetic teaching and took note of the prophet stating that God will use the voice of someone who is familiar to us to speak to us. I believe this is exactly what happened here. I pray that this was not a missed opportunity and that it happens again because nothing was sweeter to me than my mother's voice.

Additionally, in September 2011, I was worried about something one night and was tossing and turning in bed. The Lord spoke to me in a clear but matter-of-fact voice and said, "Go to sleep." I was startled at first. Afterward, I smiled and said, "Thank you, Lord." I turned over and went to sleep and slept all night. I must note here that I have had trouble sleeping since the mid-1980s after my stepfather died. I just could not sleep and was given sleep aids since that time to sleep at night. However, once the Lord told me to go to sleep, I have not had any problems since that time and do not need any more sleep aids.

Before I go to sleep at night, I cover myself and all of my family, friends, enemies, and all of our families with the blood of Jesus. I ask the Lord God to encamp His angels around us and send His warring angels before us and behind us. I have been doing this for years, and let me explain to you why. In May 2016, my daughter's allergies were bothering her one night, and she started having trouble with her blood sugar dropping. On this night, she was extremely restless before she went to sleep. Anyway, she woke up in the middle of the night and took her blood sugar reading and her temperature. Her blood sugar read 26, and her temperature was 94.5. I pray that doctors, nurses, or people in the health fields read this book because you may realize what had happened to my daughter without me saying it. The enemy attacked her during the night, and I believe that the Lord raised up my daughter from this attack. This is very frightening to realize that my daughter had left me. This is why we are to pray without ceasing. The enemy is always watching and waiting for a way to attack.

Sometime during the first of 2016, I awoke around 6:00 a.m. on a Saturday to find a sweet smell in the house. I heard my daughter in the hall and asked her, "Where are you going at this time of morning?" She answered and said she wasn't going anywhere. I then said, "Why do you have on all of that perfume?" She said that it was not her and that the smell was throughout the house. I didn't know it then, but I do believe the windows of heaven were open over my house, and the sweet incense from heaven permeated my house. Amazing? I think so.

On May 19, 2016, my daughter and I were standing in the hall after getting some trash together. My daughter started to walk down the hall, and she said, "I smell that odor again." I said, "I don't smell anything." She moved around in the hall and stopped just outside the bedroom doors and said, "It is concentrated here." She told me to stand in the same spot that she was standing. I stood there, but I didn't smell the sweet fragrance that we had smelled before. I only smelled the clear crisp fragrance of the outdoors. Moving out of that spot, I could smell the odors of the house. However, I could only smell a cleanness of the air in the one spot, while my daughter smelled the sweet fragrance of heaven.

"My sheep hear my voice, and I know them, and they follow me" (John 10:27).

I am sure a number of you reading this book don't believe me. Well, I know that these visions are true and are occurring in real time. Since I mentioned my mother again, let me share this with you. I have had trouble with the children in the neighborhood using my yard as a shortcut to get to the next street. I told them to stop several times and put up No Trespassing signs. This did not stop these children, and they continued to irritate me by coming onto my property when they thought no one was looking. One night during the summer of 2010, my mother came to me in a vision. She sighed long and deep in disgust and stated, "Leave those children alone about that yard!" I didn't know what to say. I was stunned and walked over to the window and looked out. In the vision, fresh snow was on the ground (this was the summer) and the children had made a mess of it. I said, "Mamma, look at the mess that they are making in my yard." My mother walked over to me and got in my face and said, "Leave those children alone about that yard!" I immediately said, "Yes, ma'am." My mother then disappeared. I, however, knew immediately why she had come to me. I was grieving the Holy Spirit again by getting "angry" with these children. See how easy it is to let offenses make you grieve the Holy

Spirit. My mother also came to me to warn me. She has come to me several times now to warn me or to show me things that I need to know. I think this proves that the Bible is true when it states that there are watchers and holy ones. How would my mother know these things? For me and you, we need to be careful of the things that we say, do, and think.

> *"Woe unto the world because of offences! for it must needs be that offences come; but woe to that man by whom the offence cometh!" (Matthew 18:7).*

After my mother appeared to me, it took less than a week for the children to stop using the yard as a path. Only one may sneak through within a month, but, for the most, they have stopped, and I don't see the ones who were really a problem anymore. Anyway, the older children who were bold and disregarded my statements are not in the neighborhood. Believe me, people, they stopped within a week. See what the Lord will do if you obey. They left soon after my mother appeared, and I don't know what happened to them.

Sometime in August 2009, I awoke one morning, sat up in my bed and blurted out, "222." I don't know what this means, but my daughter looked at her calendar and stated that February 22 (second month and twenty-second day) of 2010 will be on a Monday. She then looked for Rosh Hashanah in 2012 and said that it falls on a Monday also. People, believe me, I am not setting a date for the Rapture, but we thought that these dates were very interesting, and we should note it. I do not have any answers at this time. Please note that this is just me talking here. Today is February 27, 2010. Nothing peculiar happened on February 22, 2010, and I want to be clear about this. I don't know why I was given this number, and can only wait until the Lord reveals the reason to me. We can't assume anything with the Lord. He will tell us what He wants us to know. Do not guess with the Lord!

On another note, many people are talking about the "blood moons" of 2014 and 2015. The last blood moon happens on a Monday during a Shemitah year. I am not giving a date, because I am not setting them. Please get your house in order.

HAND-TO-HAND COMBAT WITH DEMONS

"Above all, taking the shield of faith, wherewith ye shall be able to quench all the fiery darts of the wicked" *(Ephesians 6:16).*

During November 2008, I decided to fast like Daniel, the prophet in the Bible. Again, Daniel fasted for twenty-one days and did not eat meat or sweet bread or drink alcohol. The devil knows when you are trying to get closer to God, and he will come at you with all that he has. Please remember that angels are fighting these demons for us and that we have to pray constantly. On November 5, 2008, while in the first week of the fast, demons came to me in a vision and tried to stab me with a long rod of some sort. During these visions, it is very difficult to wake up, get out of it, escape, or speak out at times. Therefore, I had to force the word "Jesus" through clenched teeth. In the vision, I said the name Jesus about ten times. My husband was not at home, but my daughter heard me, and said that I was calling on the name of Jesus for a good fifteen to seventeen minutes. She thought that she was hearing the television at first, but she came into my bedroom and had to shake me out of this vision. I came out of it, and she made sure that I was okay before she left the room. Afterward, I went back to sleep and found myself in the same vision. The demons came back and tried to stab me again, but I woke back up soon afterward and found myself safe. The devil really comes after you when you try to get closer to God. Don't be afraid. You must believe that the Lord is greater. For those of you who do not look at Christian television, I have heard similar occurrences like this happening to other people. Please believe me;

some of us are seeing the same things. Let me state here that I don't know of anyone who has battled these demons. I don't know why I am in this horrible battle with them, but I am. At any rate, I am not afraid because God is on my side. Let me state that these demons were the short wee people type again. I believe they are the meanest that I have encountered.

Confrontation with a Dracula-like Demon

On August 27, 2009, I fasted all day and prayed for the Lord to fill me with His power. I wanted to feel the weight of his power and stand in it. I did not feel unusual that day but felt a change in me when I went to bed that night. Moreover, I could not explain it. I had a dream that night and found myself in a vision. The vision began with me and some people that I knew going on a trip. We were in a building looking at some objects that did not seem important to me. I, in turn, wandered off from the group and found myself in a room that reminded me of a medieval castle. The room was large with an enormous fireplace, off-centered to the right and near the middle of the room. A door led outside to the right of the fireplace. Behind the fireplace and off-center to the left were two large, round recesses in the wall with circular stones placed within. Large masses of stone were on top of each circular stone. The mantle on the fireplace held a miniature black horse. As I shared this with my family, they reminded me of the four horses (white, red, black, and pale) of the book of Revelation. At any rate, this black horse had an indistinguishable object on its back. As I continued to stare at it, the horse came alive and raised its front legs as though it was about to gallop down off of the mantle. However, it did not leave the mantle. I immediately screamed, "I am in a vision." Please note that I knew and stated that I was in a vision (present tense). I have never stated that I was in a vision before. This was truly amazing. Nevertheless, I started calling out for my friends who were with me in the vision to come and help me. Suddenly, my attention was then directed to the mass on top of the first circular stone. The mass began to slowly peel away, from left to right, to reveal a man's head. It continued peeling away until a man's entire body was revealed. The man did not move, but he sinisterly grinned at me. Again, this is another grinning demon. I looked at the next stone mass, and it began to peel away in the same manner as the first. The head peeled away first and continued down to his feet. This demon got off of the circular stone and advanced toward me. I am using the words man and demon interchangeably because that is what they were. This man's teeth became canine, and he, too, had the same terrifying sinister grin. I was very afraid of this man, and I started running to the door that led outside. However, I stopped because the Lord reminded me that I had prayed that day and asked for Him to fill me with His power. We are not to fear, because fear is of Satan. I, in turn, did not want to disappoint the Lord after I asked for this power. I turned and made my way to the middle of the room and extended my hands, palms down, in front of me. The man continued to slowly advance. His teeth began to grow as he got closer. He circled me as I turned with him and continued to stare him down. He stopped and stood in front of me. The door to the outside of the room was behind him. I looked at him with confidence and told him, "I'm not afraid of you. I am filled with the power of the Lord." He reached out his right hand and touched my left hand. He immediately drew back and cowered. His face began to turn dark, and whiffs of smoke came off his face. The demon turned into a frightened little boy. Amazing. This bad demon who wanted to frighten me, turned into a frightened little baby-faced boy. The power of God is amazing. Try it for yourself. At this point, the people that I was calling came into the room, and asked, "What is wrong?" At the same moment my daughter woke me up, as she also heard me cry out in the vision. The vision of the demons reminded me that God will be with us and do what we ask. He is watching, and He is protecting us. Moreover, remember, I asked for this power. I believe that this black horse was symbolic of the economic crisis that the world will continue to face if they don't begin to love, forgive, and treat each other with kindness and respect. However, I have not gotten any message from the Lord about it and must say that this is speculation on my part. Also, I do believe that it is symbolic of the black horse of the book of Revelation. We can, at times, be the masters of our own fate. Christians of the world need to pray to our Lord and Savior Jesus Christ, just as I did, to defend against the evildoers. The black horse of Revelation may be a reference to our food or be symbolic of a spirit of a world power. To be honest, I really don't know what it represents. I think the Lord is telling me that the black horse is about to ride, and there is going to be a problem. I really don't know. Please make note of this message. Someone more gifted in prophecy may be able to answer this mystery because I can't at this time with certainty. On another note, I asked one of my brothers why this demon touched my left hand. He stated that the right hand is the hand of fellowship, and he didn't think the demon could touch it. Interesting?

I must take a moment to summarize the demons that I saw. I saw black and white men and women. All were short, not taller than my five feet two frame. I saw grayish alien-like zombie demons. I saw demons that reminded me of Dracula. I also saw the little people that were all smiles. I felt evil around these beings and can truthfully say that I do not believe in alien visitors anymore. This is my belief. I believe that these beings are demons, and they have been around all of this time to lead mankind into sin. These demons also tried to entice me to go along with them, or to get into a car with other demons to go, where?

VISION OF JESUS CHRIST

"And when he had spoken these things, while they beheld,
he was taken up; and a cloud received him out of their sight"
(Acts 1:9).

On Tuesday, November 24, 2009, I saw my only vision to date of my Lord and Savior Jesus Christ. The vision started with me and a family member in the hallway of a building. We were walking and talking when suddenly this person's face changed. The face of my relative became a face that I did not know. I was stunned and stared in disbelief at this transformation. My family member changed into someone I did not recognize. As I continued to stare, this person, who was now with me, said that he was going to hurt me. I reacted by stating, "What makes you think I am going to let that happen?" I also felt a lot of danger around this person. While I was trying to figure out who this person was, the ceiling of the building dissolved away, and a light from the sky fell around me and this person. That is when I saw a vision of Jesus completely engulfed by what appeared to be a halo of light. The light completely enclosed His body as a circle of light or as a light cloud against a black sky. I have seen pictures of Jesus standing on a cloud while ascending to heaven after His resurrection. However, this is not what I saw. I was calling the light around Jesus a halo until the Lord led me to the verses above. I saw Him enclosed or standing inside of a structure similar to a cloud of light. Let me state here that I am not trying to make the scriptures work for me, but I am trying to find something that is similar to what I saw. The cloud received Him by enclosing His entire body within it. And note, the angels said that He would return in the same manner. This is exactly what I think I saw:

the cloud covered His entire body in a perfect circular form of white light. Let me add here that one of my brothers said that it could have been a picture of how Jesus looked during the transfiguration. At any rate, I must apologize at this time because I really do not know.

> *"While he thus spake, there came a cloud, and overshadowed them: and they feared as they entered into the cloud" (Luke 9:34).*

The verse above is referring to the transfiguration. The Bible states that Jesus's countenance was altered, and his raiment was white and glistering as He spoke to Moses and Elias (Elijah). Jesus's body was transformed as he spoke to Moses, who was buried by the Lord, and Elias, who was taken from earth by the Lord. Again, Jesus, Moses, and Elias entered into a cloud. This may be similar to what I saw. Jesus appeared to be inside of an illuminated circular light.

In my vision, Jesus was standing on the moon (this is my thought— somewhere in space) while observing the earth. He was light. His clothes were white, and His face shined. Yet, He had a dark-colored wide band around His waist. I don't know if it matters, but I thought He would be dressed in gold when I saw Him. He also appeared to be very sad. At any rate, without warning, I was transported to His point of view, but just to His left and slightly behind Him. Nevertheless, I, too, was now looking back at the earth, and the vision abruptly ended. This happened two days before I was to meet someone that a relative was to introduce to me. The next day, I described the person who was in the building with me to the relative who was to introduce this person to me, and the relative's jaw dropped. I had just described the person in great detail two days before I met him. I believe the Lord gave me a warning for my family to avoid this person because the warning came true. There was definitely danger surrounding this person. I felt so blessed to have seen the Lord and to be given a vision of this person before meeting him. And yes, when I met him, he looked exactly like the person in the vision that I had seen two days before. This left me speechless.

SIGNS OF THE END-TIME

A re we not different from the generation that Jesus spoke of during His times that sought after signs? We are constantly looking for a sign from God, although Jesus stated that there will not be a sign for His generation. We have eyes that do not see. We have ears that cannot hear. This is the end-time, people. This is the time for the world to see and hear. God will not bring judgment on a nation without warning the people first. Visions, dreams, and prophesies from His saints are being fulfilled every day. All one has to do is turn on the television and hear evangelists, one after the other, saying with great urgency that the end is near. If you are not hearing about prophecy in your church, please try some of the prophecy teachers on the television.

Signs have been all around us from the year that Israel became a nation again. In fact, all of the signs that Jesus said would occur before the Rapture are in place. There is one, however, about the gospel being preached around the world. I don't know how close we are to this statement. Anyway, do you not see? Do you not believe? Do you want to stay here? We also have the most important sign in our possession: the Bible. Please read it and be prepared when the Rapture comes. Jesus gave us a commentary on these signs. Please read Matthew 24. This chapter is Jesus's discourse on His coming back and the signs of the end. Most people believe that Israel is symbolic of the fig tree, and the fig tree is back and has blossomed in the land of Israel. Also, here is a very important sign. Israel is back as a nation and has control over Jerusalem. Israel has made the land rich and fertile. And Israel is in the news practically every night.

I find the Bible to be a very fascinating book and just had to mention that Paul saw and wrote about the end-time headlines approximately two thousand years ago. Why don't people read the Bible and make note of what's happening around them?

> *This know also, that in the last days perilous times shall come.*
>
> *For men shall be lovers of their own selves, covetous, boasters, proud, blasphemers, disobedient to parents, unthankful, unholy,*
>
> *Without natural affection, trucebreakers, false accusers, incontinent, fierce, despisers of those that are good,*
>
> *Traitors, heady, highminded, lovers of pleasures more than lovers of God;*
>
> *Having a form of godliness, but denying the power thereof: from such turn away.*
>
> *For of this sort are they which creep into houses, and lead captive silly women laden with sins, led away with divers lusts (2 Timothy 3:1–6).*

Please note what the Bible says about the silly women in 2 Timothy 3:6. Today, some of them are women who love being called the *B* word and unabashedly pose nude for pictures and readily show their nakedness. And some men are proud of it. Men, it is time for you to step up and be a real man in Christ. What happened to us? They are women who don't mind listening to these vulgar lyrics in songs and responding in kind on the dance floor. People are fierce with rage. If the silly women of the world can't control themselves, men, why aren't you? Remember that Satan could sing, and this is his world. We all need to watch the songs that are on the radio. We can control that aspect of our lives. The wicked seem to prosper, but the Christians appear to be suffering.

> *"But thou hast fully known my doctrine, manner of life, purpose, faith, longsuffering, charity, patience"* (2 Timothy 3:10).

Paul states in this verse that he was long-suffering. I pray that my suffering is over because I have suffered for a long time. Why do we suffer? I don't know. However, suffer, we do.

"Yea, and all that will live godly in Christ Jesus shall suffer persecution" (2 Timothy 3:12).

All that will live godly in Christ Jesus shall suffer persecution. It is okay for you not to believe what I am saying only if you read your Bible and prove me wrong. I don't think that I have said anything that is contrary to God's word. However, I know some people are waiting to say, "She's not a prophet. She's not a preacher. Why does she feel qualified to write this book?" Even so, before you persecute me, accuse me of fraud, or mock me, get to know the Lord. I have lived a life as Job's, and pray for peace. No matter how much I am persecuted, evil people have become worse, deceiving and being deceived, according to 2 Timothy 3:13.

"But evil men and seducers shall wax worse and worse, deceiving, and being deceived" (2 Timothy 3:13).

In a time such as this, we need the Lord. There is a prayer that I say every day during my prayer time with the Lord and my praise and worship service. You, too, must take time to spend with the Lord and praise Him if you want to be connected with Him. He will talk to you and show you things that you never before could have imagined. They are Psalm 70, 71, and 91. Afterward, I read the words that are in red, which are the words that Jesus spoke. When you start to see visions, they may frighten you at first, as they did me. They were so frightening that I did not want to see them anymore. But believe me, brothers and sisters, I truly felt a separation from the Lord when I became afraid and stopped my praise and worship. Find a place in your home where you can pray in private each day. You do not have to make an altar, because we have a tendency to start idolizing the place instead of what it represents. Start now and take your communion each day.

My daily prayers are Psalm 70, 71, and 91. Afterward, I read verses in red print that represent Jesus speaking. Another note is to speak to your illnesses and declare that you are healed by Jesus's stripes.

These are my prayers of safety, my prayers of protection, and my prayers of strength for the day. I must say that I have been reading these Bible verses for more than twenty years, and also had my daughter to read them. My son does what feels comfortable to him, and that is okay. Psalm 70 and 71 were so important to us that if my daughter went to sleep without reading her verses, I would wake her up and tell her to read her Bible verses. She would always, without fail, turn to Psalm 70 and 71. Is that amazing? Can you imagine someone half asleep and always turning to the same verses?

After I have read these verses, I turn to verses in the New Testament of the Bible that have the red script. These are the words that Jesus spoke to the people. I get a visual picture of Him, either sitting or standing on a hillside. Then I read the words in red for several minutes. We must make time for the Lord in order to hear him.

During the Gulf War, I remember hearing on television that the Israeli soldiers would read Psalm 91 as a prayer of protection. I almost fell off of my chair when I heard this because after several years I had added Psalm 91 to my reading. I know that God gives us protection and guides us to that protection. For years I had been reading this verse and never knew how others were using it as their prayer of protection too.

We communicate with God through fasting and prayer. We must fast and pray constantly to keep our Holy Temples, our bodies, clean before the Lord. I do believe that by fasting and praying daily, I was allowed to see these visions and dreams. We must fast and pray on a regular basis. This is the way to communicate with God. He loves for us to talk to Him, and He loves to interact with us.

A Message to People
Who Are in Power

I have a message for owners of companies. It is important that owners of companies throughout the world have a plan in place to quell unfair labor issues of any kind in the workplace because a number of people suffer in the workplace. When the Lord looks at us, He looks at His children that He painted different colors. We have different names, religions, and ambitions. However, all Christians are His children: this I know. Those who profess to be His children and take His name as Christians and who own these companies are to be good stewards of the things that the Lord has given them. Affirmative action helped a number of people who are my age to get better jobs, but look at the number of class-action lawsuits that popped up after affirmative action was modified. Affirmative action worked well for people who were my age who went to work for the government. Most of my friends from college who worked for the government are now retired with full benefits. With affirmative action, some people got nice jobs in private industries, too, but little to no promotions and pay raises to equal their counterparts. If we love one another, I am sure that we would treat each other fairly. If the treatment of employees is important to God, all employers should take notice.

Let me note that I was sitting at my desk while at work one day, and the Lord spoke to me. He told me, "Type up everything that you have done." I was horrified. The Lord spoke to me, and I started asking: What was that? Who said that? And, what is going on? I said some other things, but I don't remember them at this time. I couldn't wait to get home and tell my mother and family. Anyway, the Lord repeated the same thing while I was at work for about a week. Therefore, I gathered my files and put them on the end of my desk and said, "Okay, Lord, I'm taking everything home and typing it up. The Lord stated once and only once, "Do not take them home." Now, I was beyond frightened. I asked the Lord why. He did not answer. I said, "Lord, if I type this here, someone will see me and ask what I am doing." He did not answer. At any rate, I was dumbfounded. I waited a couple of days and started to type. Someone did come by and ask questions, but I didn't answer and kept typing. This happened about a month before Christmas. When I came back to work from the Christmas and New Year holidays, I found out that someone had gotten a promotion over me, but I could show the work that I had done.

This is all that I'm going to say about this because I had more in this manuscript, but the Lord told me to take it out. I believe He doesn't want people to concentrate on me and my problem, but to be aware that this is an issue with Him. The Lord watches, and He knows. At any rate, the Lord said that He was in charge. The very next week after I deleted the information that He wanted out, the company lost a lawsuit, and I remembered that the Lord stated that He was in charge.

> *"But he that knew not, and did commit things worthy of stripes, shall be beaten with few stripes. For unto whomsoever much is given, of him shall be much required: and to whom men have committed much, of him they will ask the more"* *(Luke 12:48).*

To whom the word or knowledge of the Lord is given, much is required of him to get that message out. I am trying to get word of my visions and dreams to all believers and unbelievers. I don't think the verse above needs any explanation. Much has been given and much is required. Do you hear that, Mr. CEO? It is very clear to understand the meaning. Please note a verse from Malachi: The Lord is watching those who oppress the hireling in his wages too. We are only seeing the beginning of things to come.

> *"And I will come near to you to judgment; and I will be a swift witness against the sorcerers, and against the adulterers, and against false swearers, and against those that oppress the hireling in his wages, the widow, and the fatherless, and that*

> *turn aside the stranger from his right, and fear not me, saith*
> *the LORD of hosts" (Malachi 3:5).*

The message from Malachi is unambiguous, and yet confounding when I look at it. I do not remember looking for this verse or writing it. Again, I believe that I was led to it by the Lord. Employers who oppress the hireling in his wages are in danger of a judgment akin to that that is waiting for those mentioned above. When you cheat people of their wages and promotions, you are also cheating God out of His tithes. You are cutting into the tithes that that person could be giving to the building up of God's kingdom. Men conquer and seek to change people to be more like them or to eliminate them altogether. The people of the world seek to conquer and transform people to conform to their religions and ways of thought. If people were fair and responsible, affirmative action would never have been passed into law. It would not have been needed. Women and minorities at most companies fared well to get jobs because of affirmative action, but ceased to be acknowledged after affirmative action was modified. No oversights were in place to make sure that people were treated fairly in most companies. There was no one to say, "Treat people with respect and treat them fairly." However, someone is looking beyond the veil. God sees, and He knows.

Again, I did not look for this verse in Malachi. I think the Lord wanted me to write this for all to take notice. The Lord knows when people are being unfair, and He is holding someone accountable. Remember—the Lord will seek His revenge. Most of us are in danger of the judgment of the Lord. According to the Bible, a few people may be spared.

> *"Behold, the hire of the labourers who have reaped down*
> *your fields, which is of you kept back by fraud, crieth: and*
> *the cries of them which have reaped are entered into the ears*
> *of the Lord of sabaoth" (James 5:4).*

People are not pawns for others to play with their feelings, their livelihoods, or their families. Employers at the corporate level are failing the masses. There should be some accountability here on earth for the treatment of your employees before you have to give an account in heaven.

Some employees have been paid minimum wages for years, or, to put it plainly, the bare minimum. They have been passed over for promotions and raises often throughout the years. An important message is to understand that the Lord is also being cheated of His tithes and offerings when people are cheated out of their wages. Dear people, this message came directly from the Lord. I had no clue. When people are paid less, they have less to give to God. I did not understand where the Lord was leading me with these scriptures, but it is clear now. Please make note of this. Will a man cheat God? Believe me, someone is watching you, and it is not just the women and minorities here on earth. You were given much, and much will be required from you one day.

The trickle-down economics of the past to give to the rich and let it trickle down to the poor did not work, was never going to work, and is not godly. There is no overseer to make the program work, nor is there any accountability to anyone. Oh, praise be to God, for He sees and He hears!

As I write this book, I am making a note here. Many people are trusting in gold and silver for the last days. Surprise … surprise … James 5:1–3 states that your gold and silver (not dollars or any other currency) is cankered in the last days.

The Lord is not happy with the way laborers have been treated. Is anyone listening? Repent before it is too late. Please note the story of Lazarus and the rich man.

All of you rich men and employers who have cheated people for your gain need to know and understand the story of Lazarus. One need not worry as to where his body goes after death. In the days before Jesus died for us on the cross, bodies of believers went to Abraham's bosom, and the bodies of the lost went to hell to be tortured. There was a gulf separating the two areas. The righteous people in Abraham's bosom could not go to hell, and the people in hell could not go over to Abraham's bosom. However, they could communicate with each other. Remember the book of Enoch. Evil angels drag the souls of evil people down to the place that is prepared for them. However, after Jesus Christ's death, the dead in Christ went to paradise to be with Him. Again, did I see a vision of Paradise as it would look from space when I saw the planet in the vision? I don't know. However, in a vision that my daughter had, she also saw an area outside of the gates of heaven. My daughter actually saw a bench at heaven's gate that she had to sit on and wait for our Lord to usher her into heaven. Jesus spoke to her and told her that her sins were forgiven and told her to come in. Brothers and sisters in Christ, please be careful of the way that you treat each other. Let's prepare to see each other in heaven.

The Lord has shown me and my daughter much. We have heard and seen astonishing and beautiful things. For us to have heard and seen, we were privileged to something so stupendous and so rewarding that we feel destined to share these things with you. It is such an honor to be found worthy to be given this opportunity to glance into the supernatural realm and to see the things that are to come.

I had a friend who passed away recently. He knew the Bible and was a treasured friend. We would sit and talk about all of the things that were happening to me and my family, and he would say, "Glenda, the devil is afraid of something that you are going to do. The Lord has a plan for you, and that lying, scheming rascal is trying his best to destroy you." I had told him on numerous occasions that I felt like Job. It seemed that every week something new would pop up on my radar screen. My life was full of turmoil. I only wanted to be with my children and family and enjoy the time that I had with them, but that was not the case. I understand that Satan knew I had a message from God, and he wanted to stop me. He did everything in his power to stop what I am revealing in this book. You name it, and my family or I lived it. I have been through the fire, and now it is time to work for my God in these last days.

The Bible has many references to visions and dreams and their association with the last days. All Christians should be attuned to God in these last days. You should be seeking Him diligently, and He will talk back to you in dreams and visions or in person. I did not know why things kept happening to me, but I did feel that God had everything in His hands.

In John 16: 33, Jesus states that the disciples will have tribulation in the world. However, they can have peace in Him because Jesus overcame the world. We find that Jesus is speaking to the disciples, but this verse can apply to Christians today. We, too, are being tested as the disciples and Christians of old. We all are having our moments of tribulation, but we know that Jesus has overcome the world and its troubles. Know that God is your salvation.

I knew that the visions that I had seen were from God. I wrote them down for you to read and prepare for the Rapture. These visions are but one of the gifts of the Holy Spirit. One night while I lay asleep, my husband told me that I was speaking in a foreign language. My daughter has also heard me speak in this language. Was this another gift that the Holy Spirit placed on me? I don't know, but I look forward to it happening while I am awake.

> *"And they were all filled with the Holy Ghost, and began to speak with other tongues, as the Spirit gave them utterance"* *(Acts 2:4–6).*

Jesus left the Holy Spirit to comfort and guide his disciples when He left earth. The Holy Spirit was poured out on His saints during Pentecost. During Pentecost, Peter was speaking in his native tongue. People from several foreign nations were there to hear him. The miracle was that Peter's message was heard by all of the people in their native language as Peter spoke in his language. This is one gift of the Holy Spirit. God's Spirit is being poured out again on His people. Why aren't more ministers operating in this gift?

Paul states that his preaching was not to entice man's wisdom, but it was a demonstration of the Spirit and of the power. The spirit was given to the disciples. They had power. Listen carefully; the body is the vessel of the Holy Spirit. The Holy Spirit lives in our earthly bodies. We need the Holy Spirit to discern what God wants us to know. We need the Holy Spirit to also operate in the supernatural of God.

Cursing and Using the Lord's Name in Vain

Also, a spirit that is not from God causes man to curse and use the Lord's name in vain. People, do you know what or who is leading you down this path? You need to know.

Is there any wonder that people are confused? Satan is the lord of this world, and he is the author of confusion. God does not cause confusion. People, stop using the Lord's name in vain. I can find no reason for profanity to be accepted. Christians, why do we let people use our Lord's name in vain? Muslims would never accept this for their God. We must fear the Lord and respect Him at all times. You cannot curse one minute and sing praises the next. It doesn't work. For all of you young people, read and understand for yourself.

It is not necessary to curse or use conduct that is shocking or inappropriate. If one wants to make a statement that is strong and meaningful, let the Holy Spirit speak for you. Christians who fear the Lord will keep His commandments. Please read and be prepared. No one can be ready for the Lord's return by cursing and using the Lord's name in vain. Why do we Christians allow this? You cannot curse someone and turn around and speak blessings out the same mouth. It just doesn't work. Fear the Lord!

The desire of the wicked shall perish, according to Psalm 112:10. Understand. Wicked people do wicked things. Sometimes good people will do wicked things. However, it's what's in one's heart that the Lord is looking at when He looks at you. The Lord is watching what comes from the heart and mouth. Most people need to tame their tongues. You cannot curse one minute, sing praises the next, and end this with a blessing.

Cursings and blessings are different. One is of God, and the other is of Satan. The two should not be found in the same mouth. The wicked shall not prosper. Again, is there any wonder that people are confused? Satan is the lord of this world, and he is the author of confusion. God does not cause confusion. Christians must begin to act more like Christ. God is not the author of confusion. It is Satan.

When I was in college, a song came out that used the Lord's name in vain. I thought this song was "hip." I had not heard anything like this. I played this record all the time. When my roommate was out, I would turn up the volume. Did I suffer for this? You bet I did. And you will too. Stop using these vile words to make a point. I believe this is a way to open up the door and let demons in on you, your family, and friends.

People curse and use vile language to get attention. They are also moving away from God the more this is done. As a young girl, I was looking at a foreign movie one day and noticed cursing in the captions. It was startling to see that people cursed in other languages. I had no clue. Is cursing a universal jargon that Satan established as an easy path to fixate on him? People the world over appear to have an obsession with cursing. Wouldn't the god of this world want his people to call on him at all times? This is an easy way to open up that door to Satan and his demons. People, know what you are doing.

A Message for Our Youth

"And they gave him threescore and ten pieces of silver out of the house of Baalberith, wherewith Abimelech hired vain and light persons, which followed him" (Judges 9:4).

"I am black, but comely, O ye daughters of Jerusalem, as the tents of Kedar, as the curtains of Solomon.

"Look not upon me, because I am black, because the sun hath looked upon me: my mother's children were angry with me; they made me the keeper of the vineyards; but mine own vineyard have I not kept" (Song of Solomon 1:5–6).

"The leprosy therefore of Naaman shall cleave unto thee, and unto thy seed for ever. And he went out from his presence a leper as white as snow" (2 Kings 5:27).

Vain light people, a black person, and a people destined forever with skin as white as snow: are these the makings of racism? It makes one wonder, what was the most prominent color of the people when the earth was formed? I really don't believe that it matters because we are to love one another as we love ourselves, regardless of the color of our skin. But man too often judge people by their skin tone. I don't know where the different races or the term began, but we are to love one another, not only those who are like us. It is a commandment of the Lord to love each other. Anyone who hates his brother is a murderer, according to 1 John 3:15.

When I think about the term "hate crimes," I naturally think about a race crime. Hatred breeds evil. People tend to hate and mistrust people who are not like them. However, in the eyes of God, were we not the descendants of a man named Adam and a woman named Eve? Would this premise stand to make us all relatives? Oh, I forgot about the flood. Consider for a moment that the flood destroyed all of mankind and animals except for Noah, his wife, and their three sons and their wives. Nevertheless, you might want to look at this and believe that we are all related. I know this fact is true and fairly well know that we are all humans: the one race that God started back with this one man, Adam.

I don't know how these people looked, but I know that within families we can have different skin tones, hair color, and eye color. We may be different on the outside, but we are still human beings. Also, be careful about the things that you say and do to your brother! If one calls his brother a fool, he is in danger of hellfire, according to Matthew 5:22. This means all of your brothers in Christ. Again, the angel told me to love and forgive. That is it!

Hate is also an ugly word that people use freely. My mother would tell us to never say "hate" and "I don't care." Hate destroys the soul of a man. How can one profess love in his heart for someone that he hates? "I don't care" is a term with which no one should be labored. A loving and caring heart should be the mainstay of your temple, which is the place where the Holy Spirit lives. Love can guide one in the day's affairs. Love can help prevent acts of crime and unholy acts that destroy the soul.

Involvement in gang activity can also perpetuate acts of violence and fill people with hate. How have we come to such desperate levels of finding new ways to hate? Now we hate others because they wear a different color of clothing or a certain kind of color. We have dropped to such lows on the register that most acts of violence don't seem insane, and we don't care until we get into trouble. Confusion is running amok, and guess who is driving the car? Satan is, not you. You are playing a game of "Who is going to get my soul?" You are playing on Satan's playground, and he is in control. Satan is taking delight in your ignorance. Some gang members have to be incarcerated to get away from the action and lose many years locked up to break free from Satan's grasp. Others are bound by the gang's intimidations or their oaths of "brotherhood." It is sad to know that people will make an oath to a gang and not to God.

Gang initiation can be a prescription to break the law. In some cases, a murder has to be committed to join. Everywhere we look, someone is preaching to stop the violence. Has anyone heard that Jesus is coming soon for His church? Does anyone remember that the gangsters and drug dealers in the movies die or go to jail forever, and, also, in real life? This is a message to the wise: Satan may have been the first gang leader. He got his gang together, and they wanted to take over heaven, but he was thrown out. Are you, also, trying to deny yourselves the hope of ever seeing heaven? Now, he is continuously planting his evil deeds in the minds of others here on earth. Think about it! Message to gangsters: get educated and read the Bible. Some of you are illiterate and go along with the crowd. Do not let the crowd lead you. You need to be led by the Word of God. Remember—the life of most gangsters is very short. Repent before it is too late. Know who you are really working for before your soul is taken to a horror where there is no hope for return.

As stated before, many people join gangs to belong. Some people need someone to follow. Think for a moment. Satan can and does use evil people to recruit his progeny. Don't go along with the crowd, because you cannot be sure who is leading the way.

As stated before, some gang members are illiterate and follow the crowd. The way to get past this is to study in school and learn while you can. We start school in kindergarten, or prekindergarten for some students. It is embarrassing to know that some people spend twelve to fourteen years in school and learn "nothing." Too many graduate without knowing how to read and write. This should not happen. Start now, and take pride in school, and learn as much as you can. You don't need a gang to make you feel important. Know where you are going.

I cringe when I hear that the world has gone mad. Yes, there may be something wrong with some people. Doctors may call it psychosis or other medical names that I don't know much about, but the real power of confusion on this earth is that old serpent, the devil. He can be the cause of many, if not all, of the problems facing mankind today. He is constantly throwing stumbling blocks in our paths and placing people in our lives that constantly offend or desire to bring us down.

One of my brothers would often say that offenses are Satan's best weapon. Within a day, try counting the number of times that someone may offend you. When thinking about it and actually making yourself aware of it, people can be pretty mean. Someone is quick to cut you off in traffic; someone may cough on you without covering his or her mouth; someone may yell at you because he or she is having a bad day; your boss may be giving you a hard time, or on and on and on … the list doesn't stop.

On the other hand, gangs use the word *respect* as their motivation to settle scores. Someone disrespects them, and they have to commit a crime to defend their manhood. Let's see. One has to commit a crime because someone did not respect him or her. Okay, so one has to disrespect oneself to get respect from someone who committed an offense or disrespected him or her. One has to disrespect to demand respect. This is somewhat of a puzzle. One's badge of honor is threatened by someone's disrespecting him or her? Hello. Notice the dichotomy. The Bible states that offenses will come. And offenses are Satan's greatest weapons. You gang members are not gods. You cannot demand respect and retaliate when you don't get it by disrespecting. Know who is pulling your strings. The god of this world is your boss.

People the world over are asking, "Why is there so much violence in the world today?" The devil and his demons know that their end is very near. That is why! They are responsible for the confusion and turmoil that is happening all over the world. Too many young people are joining gangs to belong. The very nature of most gangs is to terrorize and create mayhem. These gangs are as bad as the terrorists that we see threatening other countries. Some gangs intimidate and threaten the very survival of neighborhoods and cities. No one can live in a society that is defined by hatred and fear. And these are the messages that God's leaders are to be preaching or instructing the flock because the Lord wants to see everyone saved. Life on this earth is about good and evil. Don't be deceived, brethren.

> *"Ye shall not make any cuttings in your flesh for the dead, nor print any marks upon you: I am the LORD"* (Leviticus 19:28).

Gang members are also prone to marking their bodies, and a number of our youth are following this trend. To me, the word *marks* means tattoo marks or symbols. I was in college with people who bore cut marks on their bodies. Most of these people came from other countries. I do not want to diminish anyone's history or religious beliefs. Nevertheless, it appears that a number of gang members, athletes, and schoolchildren are using tattoos to make a statement. God stated very clearly that we are not to mark ourselves. Read the Bible and understand. Children, please read this again. Where are you going?

Some gangs can and do breed terrorism. Terrorism is just as much a threat here at home as it is abroad. These gangs use marks or symbols on their bodies to identify themselves. People are behaving just as the Bible stated that they would be in the end-times.

> *"Can a woman forget her sucking child, that she should not have compassion on the son of her womb? Yea, they may forget, yet will I not forget thee.*
>
> *"Behold, I have graven thee upon the palms of my hands; thy walls are continually before me" (Isaiah 49:15–16).*

There is no need for man to tattoo himself. The Lord has engraved us on the palms of His hands. Mothers on this earth may forget their children, but God never forgets. Mothers may abort their children and kill them here on earth. However, their souls and spirits may be in the place that I mentioned earlier. God does not forget. Where are you going?

I look around today and become weary over the young people's fascination with death. Everyone wants to be a gangster. I pose this question to the youth of today: "Do you remember that most of the gangster's characters in the movies are not real?" There is too much association with bad characters who seem to triumph for a little time in la-la land: the land of make-believe. Yes, evil people can enjoy happiness and prosperity for a moment, but the reality is that they will be caught, put in jail, or die and go to hell: it is that simple. Evil begets evil. There is never any good that can come from evil. Does an evil thought bear a good deed? I will say no! An evil thought is set forth to root out an evil deed. And evil deeds along with your good deeds are recorded. Books in heaven record our works here on earth. Will you stand before the open books to utter embarrassment, or will joy be your reward in heaven? Remember—as I stated before, there is a waiting area where people are judged after death. I saw it, and it was real.

Do you want to sit in that seat, or do you want to go straight to hell? Or should I say, do you want to be dragged down to hell by horrible-looking angels? The thought of this scares me to no end. However, it is your choice. Where are you going?

Most of the youth find joy in shocking behavior or in shocking things. The majority of the young people do not know about the preachers having bonfires to destroy some of the music in the 1970s. During that time, a large number of people had turntables in their homes. We played our vinyl records on the turntables that the disc jockeys (DJs) use now as mixers. In playing some of these records backward, my family and I heard audible demonic messages in them. They are too horrible to repeat. I daresay that with the demeaning lyrics and vile language in some music today that the underlying messages may be too horrific for anyone to sit and listen to them. Do you know what the underlying messages are in your favorite tunes? Do you ever wonder why children kill themselves after listening to some of this music? A thought for the wise: Isn't it ironic that just as we were finding these hidden messages on the vinyl records, tape cassettes and compact disks (CDs) came out pretty quickly? It makes one think.

Our children, especially, seem to be engrossed in this vile, filthy language that permeates our radio wavelengths and the CDs that are purchased by the millions. Think for a moment with me. In the beginning of the history of the Bible, Satan was an anointed angel. He was among the sons of God.

Satan has been around for a long time. He is a son of God. He is called a serpent, and he was the serpent in the Garden of Eden. He was full of wisdom. Corruption, vanity, and iniquity came to represent everything that he is. Please note, I am not a scholar, but I have a thought.

> *"They that see thee shall narrowly look upon thee, and consider thee, saying, Is this the man that made the earth to tremble, that did shake kingdoms" (Isaiah 14:16).*

In Isaiah 14:16, Satan is called a man. He is not called a serpent or a dragon. Also, from the language that is used, it appears (to me) that he is not anything special to look at anymore since his fall. It appears that people will look at him and ask with doubt, "Is this the man that made the earth to tremble, that did shake kingdoms?" For all of the people who believed his lies, I am sure their hearts will be filled with sorrow in his last hours.

> *"Thou hast been in Eden the garden of God; every precious stone was thy covering, the sardius, topaz, and the diamond, the beryl, the onyx, and the jasper, the sapphire, the emerald, and the carbuncle, and gold: the workmanship of thy tabrets and of thy pipes was prepared in thee in the day that thou wast created" (Ezekiel 28:13).*

Note that Ezekiel refers to the king of Tyrus but appears to turn his attention to Satan in Ezekiel 28:13. He states that this king was in the garden of God. He was full of wisdom and beauty. I believe that this verse describes Satan. He goes on to state, "The workmanship of thy tabrets and of thy pipes was prepared in thee in the day that thou wast [sic] created." Tabrets may be some type of musical instruments.

Pipes may refer to the windpipe (my thoughts) and thus to the sound of the voice. Anyway, I do believe that tabrets and pipes refer to Satan's musical talents. Also, one wonders why music is so profoundly perverse. This is just me thinking. However, it appears that most musicians love to push the envelope to the shocking and bizarre. If you can't sing, don't try to intimidate young minds, especially with vile language and brazen actions.

Satan was perfect in beauty. One doesn't need to wonder why people are so egotistical or narcissistic. Satan was an anointed cherub, and he laid the groundwork for his children. He and his children will not enter heaven. Nevertheless, his fall from grace has not been swift. Yours may happen suddenly. And, remember, he is nothing for the eyes to behold in the end.

> *"Thou hast defiled thy sanctuaries by the multitude of thine iniquities, by the iniquity of thy traffick; therefore will I bring forth a fire from the midst of thee, it shall devour thee, and I will bring thee to ashes upon the earth in the sight of all them that behold thee" (Ezekiel 28:18).*

Look at verse 18 above and notice the word traffick [sic]. It is ironic that drug dealers traffic in drugs. Evil people traffic in guns. Evil people are also human traffickers. Did this come directly from Satan as a means to destroy our people? There is no doubt about the evil effects that drugs are having on people. Do I need to tell all of you drug dealers and traffickers for whom you are working? Who is your leader? Satan is your leader. He was the first trafficker. Do you understand? He was a trafficker. God will bring forth a fire to devour Satan. Please know, all of you traffickers, that the same fate may be waiting for you. "What are you doing, and where are you going?"

Again, the life of drug dealers is very short. Violence floods their lives hourly, not daily. The little people are your playmates, regardless of your admission. You are playing a dangerous game, and you will be destroyed with Satan.

> *"By thy great wisdom and by thy traffick hast thou increased thy riches, and thine heart is lifted up because of thy riches" (Ezekiel 28:5).*

Again, Ezekiel states that the king of Tyrus (I believe this is an evil spirit that the king is under or Satan himself) uses traffick [sic] to gain money and power. Satan uses people like pawns here on earth to traffic for him; and, they don't know it. They are delusional and unholy. People who traffic need to stop and think about the place that they are going after they leave here. If you go to heaven, you don't need any money or riches, because they are already there. If you go to hell, you won't need any money or anything else. Therefore, are these paltry years of trafficking and working for Satan worth losing a lifetime of joy with our Lord and Savior Jesus Christ? I hesitate to ask this question. It seems to be a very clear choice for me. What about you? Note Isaiah 5:20.

> *"Woe unto them that call evil good, and good evil; that put darkness for light, and light for darkness; that put bitter for sweet, and sweet for bitter!" (Isaiah 5:20).*

Christians, let me make a point here. In these last days, people will start to call evil good and good evil; they will put darkness for light and light for darkness, and they will put bitter for sweet and sweet for bitter.

Look around you and know that this is very true, even now. Here is a note to the wise. If you have been taught all of your life that something is wrong, what has happened to make it right or good in your sight? Please be careful.

Mere humans cannot demand that laws be changed to make evil right and darkness light. If something was wrong ten, twenty, or fifty years ago, how can we make it right in the eyes of God by passing laws? Man cannot pass laws that are contrary to God's laws and consider them righteous. Let every man think for himself and read his Bible. God is looking, and He is making notes. Mortal laws cannot and will not replace the laws that are in the Bible that God gave to us for a guide.

It is up to every individual to read the Bible for himself or herself. Go to church. Begin to identify with the Lord God, Jesus Christ, and the Holy Spirit. You will be surprised at the power that you can receive from the Lord when compared to the power that evil people receive from Satan. Try God before it is too late.

CONCLUSION

Daniel the prophet was given a vision of the end-times, but he was told to close the book and not to reveal what he had seen. The vision was not for Daniel's day, because it was for the end-times, which we are now at present. Books and videos are everywhere about the end of days as we know them. Prophecy can't be taught without mentioning the book of Daniel. However, I will not try to interpret his message.

But I want to note something here. Sometimes we pray and feel that God does not hear us. Well, look at Daniel 10:12–13. Daniel prayed and fasted while he prayed but did not hear an answer for twenty-one days. The prince over the kingdom of Persia, a demon, kept the angel of the Lord from coming to Daniel. These princes of darkness are powerful enough to keep the angel of the Lord at bay for twenty-one days. Do you understand? The demon was so powerful that the Archangel Michael had to come to the angel's rescue. People, it is important that you know who your battles are with on this earth. Remember the demon that kept trying to pierce me with lances? We are in a battle. I will never forget the Dracula-like demon that was afraid of me because I was filled with the power of God. The forces of evil are very great, and they can prevent angels from coming to earth to get your prayers. Keep praying and fasting. The Lord heard Daniel on day one and sent an angel for his prayer, but the demon of Persia (Iran) would not let the angel get to Daniel. The angel fought with the demon, until Michael came to help him. It took twenty-one days from the day that Daniel first prayed for the angel to come to him. The Lord heard Daniel and sent an angel to him right away. He will hear you, too. The words that we speak are very powerful. Watch what comes out of your mouth. Remember, also, that I stated a demon tried to stab me when I was in a Daniel fast? We are in a continuous battle with the forces of evil, and the Lord allowed me to see on the other side. This is why it is necessary for me to warn you.

The words of the book of Daniel were sealed until now. The books are open. The seal has come off. Many people have written books on their interpretation of Daniel's prophecy. If you are interested, I would read at least three for comparison.

The book of Daniel is a fascinating history of prophecy and the end-times. Many books on the market explain Daniel's vision in detail. I just wanted to note that the Bible is accurate in its historical details. It's very exciting to read about prophecy that was spoken years ago and see it materialize at this time in history. Everyone should have some knowledge of Daniel's prophecies about the end-times. One should know where we are as noted by these prophesies. Please read a book on Daniel and end-time prophecy to get a better understanding of these verses. Believe me; it would take another book to explain Daniel and the way it corresponds to the book of Revelation.

It is amazing to me to realize how far most Christians are removed from the Word of God. We should be living by all of the words that are in the Bible, not the ones that we choose to complement our lives. If people know or believe in their hearts that they are being watched, I don't think that people would do some of the bad things that they are doing. Imagine, if you will, that we are on a stage, and everything that we do and say is being noted. Does this give pause to think about your actions? It did for me. As for my first vision of the Rapture, the angel knew what was in my mind and my heart because someone is watching.

I've heard that people will depart from the faith in the last days. There will be hypocrisy in the churches. There will be false gods worshipped in the churches. There will be people who don't want to rock the boat and stand up for the true gospel. In other words, there are a number of churches around, but where are the true believers?

Paul makes a statement in a letter to Timothy about the very nature of people in the end-times. "People will be heeding seducing spirits and doctrines of devils." They are full of lies. Even now, some religious sects forbid outside marriages of their people. There are, also, people of different races forbidding marriages outside of their race. There are people who don't want to hire people of different races. Some people don't want to talk to or associate with people outside of their race. People, this is not biblical. We are to be like Christ. Can man always be the decision maker for the world? The word of the Lord is our food. Read and understand for yourself. Can man pass laws to supersede the laws that God has put in place? No, man can't. Where are you going?

> *"And Miriam and Aaron spake against Moses because of the Ethiopian woman whom he had married: for he had married an Ethiopian woman"* (Numbers 12:1).

> *"And the anger of the LORD was kindled against them; and he departed.*
> *"And the cloud departed from off the tabernacle; and, behold, Miriam became leprous, white as snow: and Aaron looked upon Miriam, and, behold, she was leprous"* (Numbers 12:9–10).

Miriam and Aaron were the sister and brother of Moses. They spoke against Moses's marriage to an Ethiopian woman, and God allowed Miriam to become ill with leprosy. Leprosy was a terrible disease in those days, and the ill person had to live outside the camp. Miriam had to feel alone and frightened because of this. The Lord does not condone acts such as these. Please read your Bible. Don't be deceived. Remember—the Lord will and does send plagues.

I have heard a number of people state that they can't understand the words of the Bible. Nonetheless, this is why we need to go to church. Find a study group to help you understand the Bible. Again, I would highly recommend a number of television programs.

On another note, don't go after strange doctrines. If an act or deed was wrong in the past, congressional laws do not make them right in the future. No matter how much a group or crowd pleads to overturn doctrines that were true and biblically correct in the past, do not be deceived. Wrong things of old are still wrong today. Have faith in the Lord and believe. Jesus is our Lord.

*I marvel that ye are so soon removed from him that called
you into the grace of Christ unto another gospel:*

*Which is not another; but there be some that trouble you,
and would pervert the gospel of Christ.*

*But though we, or an angel from heaven, preach any
other gospel unto you than that which we have preached unto
you, let him be accursed.*

*As we said before, so say I now again, if any man preach
any other gospel unto you than that ye have received, let him
be accursed.*

*For do I now persuade men, or God? or do I seek to please
men? for if I yet pleased men, I should not be the servant of
Christ. (Galatians 1:6–10)*

Paul wrote in the book of Galatians about the people falling away
from the gospel as he had preached it. He states that there is no new gospel
other than the one that he, the disciples, and the angels preached. I put
this message in here because someone used it against me to say that I was
trying to preach something new. Nonetheless, I am not preaching a new
gospel. Neither am I trying to persuade you to believe the things that I am
saying. I have only tried to share with you some of the things that I saw in
dreams and visions. Also, I don't think anything that I have said is new or
contrary to what the Bible teaches. I pray now and ask the Lord God to
forgive me if I have offended Him in any way.

We are to know that a spirit of Antichrist is in the world. Every spirit
that confesses not that Jesus Christ is come in the flesh is not of God.
Watch at all times. Arm yourself with the knowledge from the words in
the Bible. Will you read your Bible and be the judge?

*"Watch ye therefore, and pray always, that ye may be
accounted worthy to escape all these things that shall come
to pass, and to stand before the Son of man" (Luke 21:36).*

After all of the things that I have seen and shared with you, I pray that
there are those among you who will believe. For those of you who still don't
believe in the Rapture, visions, or prophecy, I pray that you will love and

forgive before it is too late. And if there is not a Rapture, why would the Lord Jesus say that we would "escape" from the things that shall come? I believe that we will escape with the Rapture of the Church. The angel told me that I could have gone up in the Rapture if I had forgiveness and love in my heart, but I did not. I was waiting around for someone who had offended me to apologize. Christians don't need someone to apologize. Note the verses below. They are self-explanatory, and I will not explain them further.

> *"A false witness shall not be unpunished, and he that speaketh lies shall perish" (Proverbs 19:9).*

> *"For what shall it profit a man, if he shall gain the whole world, and lose his own soul?" (Mark 8:36).*

> *"For ye suffer fools gladly, seeing ye yourselves are wise"* (2 Corinthians 11:19).

The Lord is preparing us for an enormously blessed event that is prophesied in the Bible. Although the term Rapture is not in the Bible, the event is described in great detail, and the word Rapture has come to be used to identify this event. The time is now for everyone to hear, understand, and act in a godly manner so that we will be found worthy of the Rapture. The Rapture can be defined as the event in which Christians will be saved from an increasingly evil, dangerous, and corrupt world. Christians will be taken away from this world miraculously to be spared the horrors that will consume the whole world: horrors beyond our comprehension that will bring the world to the brink of extinction. Most Christians know and await this event with great determination. Many scoffers remain, but conversation among Bible scholars about the validity of the Rapture continues on many of the Christian channels on television. For most believers, there is a desire to be raptured by the Lord, and there is knowledge that this grand event will happen, but the sad note to all of you is this: "Not that many people are going up." This fact is one of the main messages that I was to reveal to the world. Most Christians are not prepared for the Rapture and will be left behind. Another message for all of you who will be left behind is to inform you that you need to prepare economically on a personal, local, state, and national level. Every local government should be prepared to have a central location for people to go for safety. This place should be equipped to communicate with the rest of the country without the need for satellites. This place should be fortified against thieves and vandals. Lastly, every family member or state member should be well aware of this location.

Strong messages from the Lord began to come to me while I was working at a company in North Carolina. The Lord guided me in leaving this company and let me live the horrors of a vastly changing economy. I went from being gainfully employed to living under the support of my husband. I had several lucrative businesses and was offered a partnership in a company in Africa after I left this company, but was steered away from them. And, I might add, I was terribly frustrated and did not understand why I could not get my businesses going the way that I wanted them to develop. I soon found out that I had to feel the pressure of the economic situation that was coming in order to warn others. I can state for the record that I did indeed learn a valuable lesson. I believe the Lord wanted me to feel the stress and the pain that was coming to the world in order to write about it. The prophets and disciples of old were tested also, and although I don't classify myself as a prophet, I feel that I have gone through the fire, and I gained some insight into the nature of God. I saw the total collapse of our society (after the Rapture) and experienced the economic pains, and actually saw the danger that is to come. We, as a nation, got to this position because of the greed and evil that has consumed our nation and the world. Additionally, the concerns and welfare of our brothers, neighbors, and employees have all but become lost in a self-serving idealistic world of self-preservation. We are trying to take God out of the governments, schools, and our everyday lives. Lastly, since we don't regard God as we should, we do not keep His commandments, and most people don't know them. It is time to come back to the Lord before He brings his wrath upon a corrupt world.

The world, including the United States of America (USA), has not been a good steward of the bounty that has been bestowed upon it. The USA has been blessed with wealth and has been considered to be the most powerful nation on the earth for a number of years. We are failing as Christians and are not living Christian lives. We have squandered our manufacturing base within. We have cheated employees of raises and promotions. We have allowed managers to subject employees to harsh words and actions. And we are falling into an economic crisis that is unheralded in magnitude. I saw the 2008 economic meltdown coming in 2005 and told several people about it so that they could prepare: this can be proven. It is now time for all of us to change our ways before the next meltdown.

The Lord never does anything without revealing it to his saints first. This fact is noted throughout the Bible in warnings by various prophets. The Bible is inclusive of His plan and sets the stage for the future. Preachers are preaching that the time of this world as we know it now is about to end. The Bible states that the Lord God can and does relent of acts of punishment that He may consider against people or nations; nevertheless, I believe that we are witnessing the beginning of the close of this age. And it is us who need to change. Throughout my life here on earth, I have been told that "no man will know the day or the hour that the Lord will come for His church." I have read it in the Bible many times, and I believed this with all of my heart. However, the Lord may have relented and shown me the Rapture of the church, with a day. Or did He?

Dear brothers and sisters in Jesus Christ, please read the Bible for yourselves to have a better understanding because I don't claim to have all of the answers. The people who wrote the Bible were not just doing this to have a book for people to denounce and ridicule. They prepared a message about the reasons that they believed that the Lord God of Abraham and the gospel of Jesus Christ were real, and they wrote about the things that they saw. They were the eyewitnesses to the news of their day and today. However, they could not broadcast it over the airwaves. They wrote it down for us to read and prepare for the day that we are to be presented before the Lord.

People, understand this: a number of people saw the risen Jesus Christ walk this earth again after His resurrection. And, still, people do not believe. Is there another religion that can make a statement such as this? Jesus died and knows what is on the other side. I, too, have seen the other side, and some of it is not pretty. However, Jesus came back and was seen. We should not be ignorant of this fact.

The Bible itself states that we will not know the day or the hour of the Day of the Lord, but the Lord's saints will know when it is near. Many evangelists and preachers are preaching that it is near, even at the door. Take heed and listen, if you will. The Lord lets His people know in advance of what may befall them on earth. Individuals may experience calamities and not see them coming, but major judgments that the Lord sends on His people are prophesied before they occur so that His people will have time to repent. First Corinthians 15 contains a vast amount of knowledge. Please read it.

I love 1 Corinthians 15 because Paul lays out God's plan and tells us forthright the story from Adam to Jesus Christ and the Rapture. Paul gives us so much information in this chapter that it should leave no doubt that the story from creation to now is true for believing Christians. Note that we have the same body before death, but a different one after death, for the Lord raises us to be what He has planned for us. Please note that there is one kind of flesh of men, another flesh for beasts, another for fishes, and another for birds. Is anyone listening? According to my Bible, men do not have the same flesh as beasts, fishes, or birds. We did not evolve, according to my Bible. Christians, are you listening? How did we, as a nation, get so far removed from the story of creation?

As noted in verse 40, there are celestial and terrestrial bodies. Note again that there are terrestrial bodies. What are people calling the bodies of alien intruders now? The Bible clearly states that there are terrestrial bodies. I saw these alien bodies. They are demons, not some entity that is hiding among the stars to swoop down on earth and save us one day. They are demons. Be not deceived, for a strong delusion will come one day. Who will stand before these demons and say no. You are warned.

Be mindful, as Paul says: "Flesh and blood can't inherit the kingdom of God; neither doth corruption inherit incorruption." Are any of our corrupt leaders listening out there? Paul is also very clear about sharing a mystery with us in 1 Corinthians 15:51–52 for the end-times. He states that we shall not all die, for we shall be changed, and the dead shall be raised incorruptible. This is a picture of the Rapture that Paul has stated is a mystery. It is a mystery to a number of people even to this day because some people doubt that the Rapture will occur. We shall not all die but will be changed. Our bodies will be changed from corruptible to incorruptible, and the mortal must put on immortality to be with our Lord and Savior. I saw bodies shrinking and disappearing in a moment, in the twinkling of an eye.

Paul, many prophets, and priests were given messages to deliver to the people over the course of history. Another man, named Jonah, was given a message from the Lord to take to the city of Nineveh, whose ruins are in modern-day Iraq. Jonah did not want to take the message, so he ran from the city, and much turmoil fell upon him and the people around him. He was thrown into the raging sea, swallowed by a whale, and remained there for three days, and the Lord had the whale to vomit him out onto dry land. It is then that he knew that he had to deliver the message that the Lord told him to take to Nineveh, that the city would be destroyed in forty days. However, the city's people repented, and the Lord spared Nineveh. Jonah became angry and possibly embarrassed by his prophecy. Nonetheless, the Lord demonstrated His devotion and love for people who repent. I want to add here that it is not too late for you to repent too. If it worked for the people in Jonah's day, it will work for you too.

I imagine this was an embarrassment to Jonah after he told the people that the city would be destroyed, and it wasn't. The most amazing thing is that we see an act of God's true loving kindness that He has for His people: He can and does relent from passing judgments. It can also be said that the Lord knows the end from the beginning, and He knows what He is going to do from the start. I am mentioning the book of Jonah because it is so very similar to my story. I ran from the visions that I was seeing. I wrote another book before finishing this one. I was very afraid of what people would think or say about me. However, it really doesn't matter anymore, because I know a man. His name is Jesus. Say what you will. As a small child, I would say, "Words don't hurt." Well, they don't hurt now, and I am not afraid.

As I stated before, many visions started coming to me after I saw a vision of how the Rapture will happen. The day that I saw the vision of the Rapture put me in a mind-set somewhat similar to Jonah's. At first, I could not believe that the Lord chose me to witness one of the most significant and awe-inspiring events of Christianity. The blessed hope that all Christians are so fervently awaiting to occur was witnessed by me. Thank you, Father God.

Instead of writing down the vision at that time, I decided that I needed to get my home-based business going first and then concentrate on writing this book. But I was stopped time after time with each venture that I started, until it registered with me that I needed to write this book, forget about business, and get God's message to His people.

In the past, I hesitated because I was afraid of what people would say about me. I was afraid of being called a fraud or a perpetrator of evil. It was often difficult for me to tell my story to the people that I have selected to talk to about this. At times when I talked to my siblings and friends, I looked away and avoided direct eye contact because I didn't want to be subjected to any cynical stares or distrustful glances. Nonetheless, I know what I saw, and as time gets shorter, I know that I have to share my message. Not only did I see the Rapture, I saw how it will happen, a hint as to how long it may continue, and, most importantly, I was given a day, not a date. Notice please, I am not dating the Rapture.

The Bible states that no man will know the day or the hour that the Rapture, or Day of the Lord, will occur. So the statement can be made, as the Bible has shown (or has it?), that the Lord may change His mind or, more importantly, that he knows the end from the beginning. We may, if one is to believe what I saw, have a clearer picture for believers and nonbelievers of how the Rapture will occur, as I explain from my vision. First, I look at the way that Moses and the Israelites wandered through the wilderness because they were a hardened and murmuring (gossiping and complaining) and sinful people. They were given freedom, and made it a burdensome task. God changed His mind and would not let them go into the Promised Land until that generation of people, who sinned against him, had died. Just as He changed His mind about destroying Nineveh, I saw a vision that He has, maybe, changed His mind about the Rapture by revealing how it will occur. Additionally, He may have given me a day, not the actual date, but a day that it will happen. Or did He? I don't believe anyone can state definitively how the Lord thinks or what His plan is, but I believe what the Bible states: the Lord does not change. He knows what is going to happen from the end to the beginning and the beginning to the end. It may only seem that He changes His mind. You be the judge and read for yourself.

Additionally, if people are to believe what I have stated about the Rapture happening on a Monday, they may believe and try to get their lives in order before each Monday occurs. In a time such as this, wouldn't it be nice to have as many people as possible waiting on the Rapture to occur on a Monday. They would love and forgive. They would be kind and gentle. They would be in harmony with the Lord's Word. And, most of all, it would be a start.

> *"And the* LORD *repented of the evil which he thought to do unto his people" (Exodus 32:14).*

The Bible states that the Lord repented of the evil which he thought to do in Exodus 32:14. I believe that prayers of the saints, just as the requests of Moses for leniency, bring us and our cares to the Lord, and He hears, and He answers. In addition, I do know that He loves us so much that He gives us chance after chance to repent and warning after warning to prepare for His judgments. The Lord shows us His plans through dreams and visions. I recently heard that Jesus is showing up in people's homes in the Middle East. Do you understand? He is showing up in Christian and Muslim homes. He is alive and wants the world to know of His loving grace for believers. Wouldn't it be wonderful to know all of God's plans and the exact timeline for those plans? If we did, do you believe that people would love and forgive? Some may do so only the day before the close of this age with the Rapture. However, it would be a day of living in complete accord for Christians around the world if we all knew that day when He is coming.

Again, I am very much aware that some people don't believe in the Rapture. I am also aware that there are people who are not religious and are not knowledgeable of what the Rapture is or that it will happen. This message did not come to me until I truly tried to seek the Lord by fasting and praying fervently. You, too, must seek His face by allowing a time each day to pray to hear from Him. You must fast sometimes before praying and believe in the Lord and Savior Jesus Christ. Humble yourselves and pray. The Lord will reveal his plans to His people and through His servants before He will bring any harm to the earth. This is exactly what He did in Noah's days. The people must have seen Noah building the Ark for many years. Noah probably warned some people that the earth would be overtaken by a flood. Maybe that generation of people did not believe Noah's warning until the flood came. Instead, Noah was perhaps mocked and maybe pitied as he went about his Father's work. On another note, the Lord also warned Lot before the destruction of Sodom and Gomorrah. His own sons-in-law mocked him. Therefore, Lot left Sodom with his wife and his two daughters. His sons-in-law are not mentioned anymore; therefore, we know their fate.

Praise the Lord God for revealing His plan of salvation, will you? Even though I saw people raptured, I did not see that many go up!!! Let me state this again. I did not see that many people raptured. Sadly, most of you are not going up. Right here, right now, in this space and time, as you read this; do you understand? Most of you will miss the Rapture unless you repent and believe in the Lord God Jesus Christ and forgive and love one another. This is not a grueling task. Believe me, this is very simple. The Bible is the witness of our Lord and Savior, and it has not been proven wrong. We have before us all the words and witnesses to His life and His Salvation through love. It is so much easier to love than to hate. Please, brothers and sisters in Jesus Christ, let us begin to live more like Him.

What a statement of truth to be told. The world is too full of itself. Nonbelievers abound throughout the world. Let me quote a scripture here from the book of Jude. Please note:

> "How that they told you there should be mockers in the last time, who should walk after their own ungodly lusts" (Jude 1:18).

Too many people do not believe because they are caught up in the affairs of men. They are walking in their own ungodly lusts. For them to believe in the Bible, they can't live as wickedly as they do now. They are quick to appear sensitive to ungodly principles as the norm of today. However, God's laws are true for days of old and true for today. It is time to be caught up in the affairs of God before it is too late. Let the Bible speak to you.

A messenger from heaven showed me the vision of the Rapture. When I saw the vision of the Rapture, I felt afraid; I cried, and I had to tell someone. But, most of all, I knew that I had to do what the angel of the Lord told me to do. I had to confess forgiveness and love to the people that I felt owed me an apology. Anyway, without hesitation, I knew that I had to do it that day. Now I feel compelled to relay that same vision to you, so that you may also be prepared to face our Lord and Savior on that day.

In the Mount of Olives discourse, Jesus's disciples ask Him what shall be the sign of His coming and the end of the world. Please read Matthew 24 in its entirety. It is too long to list here. However, Jesus states that there will be great tribulation. Remember—I believe there will be great tribulation after the Rapture. I believe the Rapture comes first, and the tribulation comes afterward because I witnessed a beautiful day with a deep blue sky just before the Rapture.

Again, the Rapture can happen at any time! The signs are here! The time is now. We are waiting and seeking after signs. Praise God, people, for the signs are here. Jesus referred to His generation as a wicked and adulterous generation that seeketh after a sign. A number of preachers and teachers of prophecy can explain the end-time events better than me. However, the signs are here, and they have given the message, and the message is that the Rapture can occur at any time. Will you be ready when the Rapture occurs? If not, I suggest that you, your loved ones, and governments of the world make plans for all who are destined to be left behind. Stock up on drinking water and supplies. Know how to contact family members. Get a shortwave radio. Have a safe place for everyone to meet. I assure you that all of you will not make it there because of all of the horrible things that will be taking place during that time. I am an eyewitness to those events. All cities need to have a disaster plan ready. This is an economic and safety issue that all nations must be prepared for in that day. It is so sad to think that so many people will be caught here on earth unprepared. Be wise and prepare for the Rapture of the church. Get your family members together and be ready to go up instead of being left behind. Will you be ready like the virgins who had their oil and were waiting for the bridegroom in the book of Matthew? Or will you be left like the virgins who were not prepared?

For those of you saints who will not heed the words of the Lord and forgive and love, you will be left here on earth during the great and horrible Day of the Lord that I believe comes after the Rapture. You will not hear the sound of the shofar. You may see the angel as he blows the shofar: that, I don't know. However, I do know that for those of us who do not go up in the Rapture, the sound of the shofar will not be heard. And all who understand that the Rapture has taken place will know immediately what has happened, but it will be too late. I can't repeat this fact enough. Forgive and love everyone while you can. Stop listening to the vicious hatemongers who deny the Rapture, or Christ, for that matter. My understanding is this: the Rapture occurs, the world is in total chaos afterward, the Antichrist is revealed, people will make an allegiance to him, Antichrist signs a seven-year treaty with Israel, he breaks it after three and half years, the tribulation begins and will last for three and a half years, and Jesus Christ will return at the end of the last three and a half years from the beginning of the tribulation and destroy the Antichrist, and a new heaven and earth will appear with a new Jerusalem. Everyone should know that the tribulation will last three and a half years from the midpoint of Daniel's seventieth week, or seven years. Please turn from your wicked ways and love.

The Bible is a history for Christians and a guide for how we should live. It takes us from the beginning of days to the end of days. The Lord God of Abraham, Isaac, and Jacob is the only God, and Jesus Christ is His Son. We are to live according to His plans as they are set forth in the Bible. These are unchanging words that the Lord has laid out for us. His words are just and true for all believing Christians.

Please note how the prophets of old were called and prepared to dream dreams and see visions. The Lord can speak to you or come to you in dreams and visions too. I don't know if there is a distinct difference between dreams and visions. You may want to investigate this later. Remember—I am not a scholar on these issues. I do, however, know when I am experiencing dreams and visions from the Lord, or the other side. Dreams are sporadic, and visions are very linear and orderly.

I don't know why this was placed on my heart, but I have to write it down. The government and private employers have cheated people when it comes to pay and retirement. What happened to our Social Security payments that were to benefit us during our retirement? Why do we have to fight for it, or pay an attorney to help us get these benefits when we need them? On the other hand, politicians have maintained a more than decent plan for themselves. The age of retirement keeps increasing, while the stress, pay, and promotions on jobs continue to be unfairly leveled. Evidently, the God of Abraham, Isaac, and Jacob is disturbed by the way employers deal with their employees. If this fact was not so, the Lord would not have spoken to me to warn me that someone was getting a promotion over me. He wanted me to be able to show that I was deserving of a promotion too. This is a question to be answered: How many employers are fair to their employees in promotions and raises? Additionally, how many employers create a pleasant environment for their employees to work? Lastly, how many employers are treating their employees with a Christ-like love? God cares, and He is looking.

What has happened to the land of freedom? What is going to happen to America? I don't know. But I do know that most of her people have not earned the right to be included in the Rapture. I cannot stress the fact enough that I didn't see that many people going up in the Rapture. Therefore, where do you go from here, America? Is it fair to bring the jobs back that were shipped to other countries and give them back to our citizens who need them? Is it fair to have accumulated so much wealth in a few classes of people and sit back and watch people struggle, go hungry, or die because of a lack of medical care or clean water? When will God's people demand that godly and sound judgment return to our judicial system, and let that trickle down to the states, cities, towns, and other countries that are open to receiving it? I saw the economy becoming a problem for America back in 2005 during a vision. I saw that safety would be a problem for America in the future. I knew, without an economist telling me, that trickle-down economics would not work when it was purposed. I have seen the black horse preparing to ride. I believe something is going to happen to our food. The loss of bee colonies and the oil spill in the Gulf on June 8, 2010, may be a prelude. Please wake up, America. Christian brothers and sisters, please start asserting your faith. Please start to forgive and love. Please treat people fairly, for you know not when you are entertaining angels. Please be mindful of your thoughts and what you say. Please get your house in order because the Rapture is coming soon, and someone is watching us from beyond the veil.

America can be the beginning of a Pentecostal movement. Another Azusa Street is needed to bring America back to godly principles. Once it starts here, we can then spread out among the nations. Everyone needs to come back to God before it is too late. Let the offenses come. There is no doubt in my mind that they will come. We, however, should be strong in these times to stand against Satan and his demons. I withstood the demon attacks against me by asking the Lord to fill me with His power. His power is the Holy Spirit. The demons bow to the name of Jesus. They flee in horror when they know who you are in the Lord. This is why everyone should pray without ceasing. Satan hates prayer. He and his demons are constantly looking for bodies to possess.

Again, we are being watched while here on earth from beyond the veil. The angel and my mother would not have known what was happening to me if they did not see it by observing me or hearing me or knowing my thoughts. Someone is watching all of our actions, and they are recorded in the books in heaven. These books will be opened one day, and your life's story will be there for everyone to know. How do you want to be judged? It is that simple. You make the choice before it is too late.

There is also a world beyond the veil that is populated by demons. The beings that I saw can only be categorized as demons, not aliens. They are black, white, male, female, and alien-like (not alien). There are also the little people who I believe give us the most challenges. Please know who is watching and who you are performing for on earth. Yes, the world is a stage.

I realize that many of you reading this book will not believe me, especially preachers. I ask you, how many souls do you save on Sunday? Are people being healed by the laying on of hands in your services by the elders of the church? Are you preaching the Revelation of Jesus Christ? If you are not doing these things, then don't mock me. I am about my Father's business.

Please remember that the Lord tells us that that day of the Rapture should not overtake us as a thief, if we love Him and believe on Him! As Christians, we are to be prepared; we are to know when the day is near, and it should not come as a surprise. The Lord demands us to know the time that we are in. Also, it is important that we prepare as a nation to go up when our Lord comes for His church. America, please be prepared. At this time, Christians are accepting too many doctrines that are not biblical. Please make a change before it is too late. Many people will be left here, and they are not prepared for that either. Many people will die after the

Rapture. Many homes will not be safe. Most people are not prepared to go up in the Rapture, and most are not prepared to stay here. This is a truth.

The children of Israel were in bondage in Egypt. The Lord God delivered them by sending a prophet named Moses. Many people are in bondage here on earth. Some are bound by incidents of their own making. Some are bound by people. Some are bound by Satan. The main question is, How does one break free? For one, education is a strong device. Educate yourself. Go to school to learn. Have goals in life. Students who refuse to learn in school are the ones who are forever reaching to attain goals that would have been easier to conquer with the knowledge that was available to them for the first eighteen years of their lives. Know where you want to go and end up in your life. Prepare for your future. Most youngsters think it is cool not to study while given the opportunity. Please know your deceiver because it is very hard to get anywhere in life without taking full advantage of the educational system that we have in America. While you are learning, give God a try. Make Him your Lord and Master. Heaven is waiting for you too.

Our harvest is with the Lord. Let no man deceive you. For every man is to bear one another's burdens. God is not mocked. Whatever we sow, we shall reap. If we sow meanness and cruelty, we will reap the same. If we sow love, we can, but not always, reap the same. Learn God's commandments and live by them each day. We need to learn the word of God, believe in the word of God, and live by the word of God. We need to keep the word of God in our hearts. His word is the seed that we receive. Satan is sitting in the wings to take the word from those of us who do not nurture it and live by it. A veil covers the earth and allows Satan and his demons to watch and prepare to pounce on us if we open the door to him. Conversely, God, the Holy Spirit, and angels are watching also. Since we know that we are being watched, shouldn't we act like we care about who is doing the watching?

In days such as these, it is sad to know that our children are looking for power. They look to satanic forces and gangs. Children are to know that Satan wants them. He goes after children when they are young and vulnerable. Little children, teens, and adults should not be in bondage to Satan and his wiles. Give up on the quest for power down here, unless you are seeking the power of the Holy Spirit. Don't be led astray by the first trafficker and his minions. Know what doors you are opening, and let it be the doors to heaven. There is definitely a heaven and a hell. Where are you going?

I don't know why we have to suffer here on earth. It is a good thing to suffer for Christ because we know where we are going. If, on the other hand, you are suffering for Satan, please know that you are preparing to meet him when you die, if not sooner. Do not be deceived. He comes when you take mind-altering drugs. He comes when you consume too much alcohol. He comes at times when you are most helpless. Most of you have seen and heard him, even though you don't want to admit it. Know who is in control of your life. Sometimes, it is not you. There are many books on heaven and hell. Read and understand who you are and where you are headed. We have the freedom in America to read any book that we want. This is not a choice for people in many countries. You owe it to yourself to do your own research.

The book of Revelation was written by John, who is considered to be a disciple of Jesus Christ. This is a belief of most scholars, but I have read and witnessed a number of theologians using philosophy to try to explain biblical theory and give authorship to an unknown or to someone named John. You read and do the research. Anyway, John was taken to heaven in a vision and shown the judgments that will come upon the earth. He gives us a firsthand knowledge of the throne of God. He describes some of the wonderful things that are in heaven and gives us a history lesson about the end-times and the glorious return of our Lord, Jesus Christ.

I tried to think about the last time I heard a preacher giving a sermon on the book of Revelation, and I could not recall any. Many people are afraid of the book of Revelation and most do not understand it. It is overwhelming when I hear people say that they are Christians, but they don't want to hear or preach on the book of Revelation. How can we as Christians believe parts of the Bible and preach on those subjects and disregard the book of Revelation as something totally symbolic of its true meaning? This book is the Revelation of Jesus Christ. It is the revealing of what is to occur on earth in the last days with the return of Jesus Christ and His reign on earth.

Many people have written books about the book of Revelation and its meaning. I suggest you read at least three of them for an explanation because I will not try to explain anything here. John describes the events in this book as a scholar with a story to tell. The Lord permits him to look into the future and explain events using his words to describe latter-day occurrences. Therefore, the symbols may seem peculiar, but here is a man who is describing events taking place almost two thousand years in the future with words used in the first century. I want you to receive a blessing from God for reading this book. It is the only book in the Bible that comes with a blessing. Please read it and be blessed. Amen, and amen.

References

All of the Bible references were taken from the following on Biblegateway.com (spellings and verses were not changed or modified).

BibleGateway.com is © Copyright 1995–2007
Gospel Communications International

Version Information

In 1604, King James I of England authorized that a new translation of the Bible into English be started. It was finished in 1611, just 85 years after the first translation of the New Testament into English appeared (Tyndale, 1526). The Authorized Version, or King James Version, quickly became the standard for English-speaking Protestants. Its flowing language and prose rhythm has had a profound influence on the literature of the past 300 years. The King James Version present on the Bible Gateway matches the 1987 printing. The KJV is public domain in the United States.

prophecyinthenews.com
Prophecy in the News magazine: February 2009, March 2009, and July 2010
Dr. J. R. Church and Gary Stearman

Printed in the United States
By Bookmasters